Short Stories and
Poems to Boot!

Short Stories and Poems to Boot!

Gabriel Alfonso Rincon-Mora

VANTAGE PRESS
New York

Cover design by Ximena Cajias

FIRST EDITION

Copyright © 2001 by Gabriel Alfonso Rincon-Mora

Published by Vantage Press, Inc.
516 West 34th Street, New York, New York 10001

Manufactured in the United States of America
ISBN: 0-533-13735-7

Library of Congress Catalog Card No.: 00-92308

0 9 8 7 6 5 4 3 2 1

For the freedom and inspiration to bare it all!

Contents

About the Author

Gabriel Alfonso Rincon-Mora was born in Caracas, Venezuela, on January 30, 1972, to Gilberto and Gladys M. Rincon. In 1983, at the age of eleven, his family moved from Maracay, Venezuela, to North Miami Beach, Florida, in the United States. After some struggle with adjusting to a new language and culture, he was accepted into the *National Junior Honor Society*. He joined the soccer team that first year and continued to play soccer throughout high school in the varsity soccer team. While attending high school, he worked part-time at a plumbing supply store to pay for his personal expenses as well as to save money to attend college. In the summer of 1988, he was selected to work for the *University of Miami* at the *Physical Chemistry Oceanographic Laboratory* in Key Biscayne, Florida. He was also selected to work in the *Electrical Engineering Laboratory* at *Florida International University* the following school year, his senior year of high school. He graduated from high school with several honors and in the top two percent of a class of approximately 950–1000 students. Among other honors, he was awarded a *Certificate for scholastic excellence in Mathematics,* a *Certificate for scholastic excellence in Science,* and the *Presidential Academic Fitness Award* signed by President George Bush. He became the recipient of three scholarships as a result: *Faculty Scholars* from *Florida International University, Florida Undergraduate Scholars* from the *State of Florida,* and the *Insignis Scholarship* from the *University of Detroit.*

He chose to attend an in-state university, *Florida International University* (FIU). Throughout his college years, he continued to work part-time, between 20 and 30 hours per week, to supplement his scholarship stipend and to save money to ultimately attend graduate school. For the last year and a half, he worked for a Patent Law Firm as an Accounting Assistant and a Prior Art Researcher. He finished his *Bachelor of Science* degree in *Electrical Engineering* in three years and four months, with *High Honors* and at the top of his class. His area of specialization was *Biomedical Engineering.* He was in the *Florida International University Dean's List* and he was given *Honorary Award Recognition* in the *National Dean's List* and *Honorable Mention* by the *National Science Foundation.*

In January of 1993, he started his graduate program at *Georgia Institute of Techology* (*Georgia Tech*) in Atlanta, Georgia. Unfortunately, he had to pay out-of-state tuition the first two quarters he attended the institute. He used his savings toward this end, with the help of student loans. He worked a co-op period for *Northern Telecom* in Atlanta, Georgia, during the summer of 1993 to supplement his income and to attain some professional experience. Shortly after, he was offered a research assistantship that would pay for tuition as well as a modest stipend.

Subsequent to earning his *Masters of Science* degree in *Electrical Engineering* with a *Minor in Mathematics,* he worked a co-op period of six months with *Texas Instruments* (TI), before going back to school to pursue his *Ph.D.* in *Electrical Engineering.* His work led to the product release of a power management IC for cellular phones and a fast TTL-input (transistor-transistor-logic-input) driver family, two products that are still actively sold in the marketplace. Four patents resulted from that work. A permanent full- time position was extended to him afterwards, which he declined to pursue his Ph.D. at Georgia Tech. The *Standard Linear Group* at TI then decided to fund and to sponsor Gabriel, a Ph.D. candidate, for the rest of his schooling career.

His area of research was *Low Voltage Micro-Power Low*

Dropout Regulators (LDOs), a brand new area of research. In December of 1996, he finished his program and earned his *Ph.D.* degree. He was named *"Outstanding Ph.D. Graduate."* He earned both, *MSEE* and *Ph.D.* graduate degrees, in about three years and three months, not including the co-op periods. He started working full-time for Texas Instruments on January 1997, as a Design Engineer, now a Senior Design Engineer, Design Team Leader, and Member of Group Technical Staff. In 1999, he was appointed Adjunct Professor for Georgia Tech. His work at TI has led to the successful release of many product lines in the field of integrated circuits, power management products in particular, which are already in the marketplace in products like cellular phones, pagers, laptop computers, desktop computers, etc. He currently also serves as a technical advisor for his branch and TI as a whole.

Today, Dr. Rincon-Mora is the author of a textbook to be published by IEEE Press jointly with John Wiley and Sons in 2001 (*Voltage References: From Diodes to Precision High-Order Bandgap Circuits*), the author of several journal publications, the inventor of numerous patents, and the designer of many products sold throughout the world. One of his designs, in fact, was featured on the cover of *Electronic Design,* a well-respected trade publication, and featured on *EDN's Top 100 Products* for 1998. For his work and contributions to the field of engineering, the Society of Professional Hispanic Engineers (SHPE) honored him with the *National Hispanic in Technology Award* in early 2000. For his contributions to the field of analog integrated circuit design, he was inducted into Georgia Tech's *Council of Outstanding Young Engineering Alumni.* He was also among the list of *The 100 Most Influential Hispanics,* as voted by Hispanic Business magazine (a national magazine). For his vision and impact in the engineering field, Florida International University honored him with the *Charles E. Perry Visionary Award.* The Lieutenant Governor of California also honored him with a *Commendation Certificate* for his contributions to the field and society as a whole. He has been on the cover of such publications like *La Fuente* (a local magazine owned by the Dallas Morning News), *SHPE* (the Official Magazine of SHPE), and *Hispanic Business.* Additionally, he has also been featured on *EE Times* (a trade magazine) and *Planet Analog* (a web publication), not to mention several other newspapers and publications. He is a Senior Member of the Institute of Electrical and Electronics Engineers (IEEE), a member of the Society of Professional Hispanic Engineers (SPHE), Phi Kappa Phi, Tau Beta Pi, and Eta Kappa Nu.

Writing has been one of Gabriel's passions. He likes, most of all, reading and writing short stories and poems. His inspiration is derived from his own experiences. Many of his poems have been published in book anthologies, not to mention various sources through the Internet. He also enjoys traveling throughout the world, from places like Luxor, Egypt, and Teotihuacan, Mexico, to Taichung, Republic of China, and St. Kitts in the French West Indies. He also enjoys playing competitive sports and has done so throughout most of his life.

Short Stories and
Poems to Boot!

SHORT STORIES

Plummeting into the Abyss!

What better sensation is there than flying freely across the blue velvet sky? To dive into white cottonlike clouds where the only audible sound is derived from the wind as it breathes through the skin. With what jealousy have I always seen pelicans and eagles masterfully manage and control torrential wind currents to carry them across open land and turbulent waters? This is my dream: to float among birds and clouds and thusly partake in the thrill of flight! Technology has rewarded us with that privilege, not quite in the same way as the aces in the sky but certainly above ground and through the clouds like them. The airplane is the vehicle that allows us to do just that. Unfortunately, a breezeless cabin robs us of the wind and the chronic sound of engines pollutes the stillness of the quiet heavens. Though the experience transcends terrestrial two-dimensional transportation, its sensation only leaves me with appetite for more. Popular freefall rides at carnivals and county fairs are invigorating and quite enjoyable but far too short and much too close to ground to justifiably call it flying. The only drink that will quench this growing thirst can only be the ultimate, which is plunging into empty space without the aid of the noisy mechanical marvels of our time. The answer is *SKYDIVING!*

One Sunday morning I prepared myself for just that.

"Hey, Jim! Are we ready for some skydiving today?"

Jim is a friend whose experience in skydiving surpasses my

years of existence on this planet! He started skydiving in the Army and continued to do it as a sport many years since. He is now fifty-one years old and still skydives at least once a month. That morning, after having breakfast, we drove for about an hour to an hour and a quarter to get to the "*drop zone*" in Gainesville, Texas. We were driving north from Dallas. It was a little breezy that day, and the sky showered us with scattered white clouds. We arrived at the small airport around a quarter past eleven o'clock in the morning. There were only two or three visible hangers in the airport. One single propeller and two twin-propeller airplanes were parked at the head of the runway just outside of the hangers.

We walked into a half-empty hanger the size of three-quarters of a basketball court. A girl in her twenties was rolling up a parachute into a small backpack; she was packing it. When she finished, she started on another one, apparently that was her job. Another gal, in her thirties, was carefully and slowly folding her chute. She was obviously packing her own chute to make a dive.

"What choices do I have in terms of skydiving for the first time?" I asked the older woman behind the desk.

"You can do a *Tandem* jump or an *IAD* jump. However, IAD requires a full day of training starting at around nine o'clock in the morning, and it is already past eleven."

"IAD?" I repeated with a questionable tone.

"Yes, that's Instructor Assisted Deployment!"

"I will do the Tandem then!"

In a Tandem jump, the student is attached to an instructor whose backpack is equipped with a parachute big enough to carry the weight of two. Before the jump, though, the student goes through ground school, which prepares him for the fifty-second freefall ride and for the deployment of the parachute. In-flight, after the ripcord is pulled and the parachute opens, the student is given the opportunity to assist the instructor in guiding the fall to safe landing.

My instructor's name was Mike. He had all sorts of certification with over thirty-plus years of experience. Jim assured me that Mike's credentials were on the up-and-up: "U.S. Parachute Association Instructor/Examiner, FAA Certified Master parachute Rigger, and FAA Certified Flight Instructor." Mike, like Jim, had also started skydiving in the Army. With all these introductions said, Mike gave me about half an hour's worth of training on the ground. He introduced me to all the equipment, gave me some instructions to follow, and coached me in the art of a proper plane exit. He also mentioned that part of my training would be conducted in the air while we dropped. I would be able to deploy my own chute, under the supervision of the Tandem Master of course, as well as practice turning, slowing down, and finally landing.

I was given a set of overalls, a helmet, a pair of goggles, and a harness. Our load consisted of nine to ten skydivers, including myself that is. We all got into the twin propeller plane and started our taxi. It felt as though we were riding a bus. It was a shallow and narrow cargo bay with worn-out carpeting. We all sat on the floor in two files and faced each other's backpacks. I sat in front of my instructor, and the thirty-something-year old woman sat between my legs in front of me. Jim was in the other file in a similar configuration. During takeoff, we all leaned towards the front of the aircraft to shift the weight and help the plane take off the ground. And off we went! We ascended slowly. I watched the airport as it went into the distance. At this point, we had to yell to overcome the noise of the engines. Once above ground, we redistributed the weight evenly and opened the translucent hatch about a foot to allow air into the plane. It was a hot July day! The ride was cozy and the fact that *I did not know anybody from Adam,* except Jim that is, did not prevent the group from sharing and celebrating the experience with me. I felt comfortable and among friends. They all eagerly welcomed me with joy into the sport! A sort of fraternity developed as we climbed into the heavens.

We made long wide circles while rising. We were going to ascend to *thirteen thousand feet* above ground before we jumped out of the plane. I had an altimeter strapped across my chest, and I checked it periodically. The plane ride was somewhat bumpy and shaky. We hit a small air pocket in the way. I was checking my altimeter at two thousand feet when, quite suddenly, the cabin became dark. The once-unveiled clear blue sky abruptly hid behind a thick wave of dark black clouds. Unexpected thunderstorms are not uncommon in this area, also widely known as *Tornado Alley.*

"We cannot jump through those clouds like that?" Mike said in a low tone.

Thunder was then heard in the background. I clasped to the side of the seatless plane just by the window when I heard yet another commanding voice, the source of which I do not know: "WE HAVE TO JUMP NOW!" The tone alarmed me, of course. All of us started placing our helmets on. The fuzz around the plane was intense! The coolness yet rapid reaction of the crew to this unexpected event was dreary and surreal. I felt my back pulled into Mike, the Tandem Master. He was strapping me into his harness. We all got up with our knees buckled and back slightly bent. The plane shook in reaction to our brisk movements. I do not know what was so wrong with the plane that propelled this response from the group, but I was already too deep into it to be able to back out and too much of a novice to voice an opinion.

One of the parachuters whose name I do not know opened the hatch all the way and started waving us to it. Then, the rest of the group started darting out of the plane, one by one in a quick succession. The small plane bounced as its cargo was jettisoned, a load at a time. I was speechless and somewhat numb at this point. Since I was the first one to get into the plane, I was the last one to exit, with Mike that is. It was my turn to approach the hatch, and as I did it, I saw the last diver plunge into the open air, head first, and quickly float away. I stepped onto the edge and looked out. What a sight! The wing was to my right, the plane behind me, and gushing air was streaking across my face like a hurricane. It felt a little cold too. We then dove into the dead of silence! The drastic sound of the engine was absent, and all I could hear was the wind as it squeezed between the folds of my overalls and gear. I was falling into a endless bottomless abyss. All my senses were stimulated to the brink of numbness. Adrenaline drowned and clogged every pore of my soul. My extended arms and legs lagged behind me as I fell through the vacuum. I lost complete perception of time and complete sense of history. I was no longer a citizen but a free soul plummeting through the sky. My wings were my arms and legs, which allowed me to change course and speed. *I was flying!* My whole body rested on a bed of air.

The thought of approaching ground at a low altitude without an open parachute suddenly struck me. This is when I felt all sorts of movements on my back as Mike quickly proceeded to try to deploy the chute. I suddenly felt a tremendous force hold me and pull me up. The parachute opened! We were still falling fast, though! At a much slower rate but fast nonetheless. I could only hear a soft whisper as the ground rapidly approached. "It's too late," I sighed with eyes wide-open and legs down and out, awaiting the inevitable.

"Okay. Put your goggles underneath your helmet!"

"Ah? . . . What? . . . Ohh! Yeah, yeah! Got it. I'm ready!"

"We're at thirteen thousand feet; we are ready to unload! Go, go, go, go!"

Blood!

As far as days go, this was a good old "middle of the road" summer day. Gilberto, a law-abiding family man, was driving his two boys to get a much-dreaded but needed haircut. The place was *Maracay,* a city in *Venezuela,* and the period was sometime in the late nineteen seventies. The town was not large, but it was big enough to house the hustle and bustle of an industrious urbanized community. Street vendors of all sorts populated the picturesque streets of *El Centro,* downtown. Crowded mini-vans without air conditioning were the main source of public transportation, and many people used them. In fact, they were so accessible and popular that a fifteen-minute wait, or less, assured a citizen a ride, a trip that would cost him one *Bolivar,* the local currency.

Raspados were one of the boys' favorite treats. A Raspado consisted of crushed ice served on a conical paper cup, liquid flavoring, and sweet condensed milk. There were several flavors available, but the preferred one by the boys was *Colita,* a strawberrylike substance. This particular day, Gilberto bought Raspados for his two sons, one for each. It is no surprise that the flavor they picked was Colita. Having to run some errands, the boys enjoyed their treat while riding in their dad's Ford, a powerful blue *Fairlane 500.*

While gradually decelerating to stop at a transitioning traffic light, when it changed from yellow to red, a big flesh-toned Ford LTD, out of nowhere, suddenly cut them off, forcing Gilberto to abruptly slam on the breaks. The cars' bumpers barely missed each other! It was with great surprise, however likely, that

Gilberto, upon turning his head, saw blood in his younger son's face. "WHAT?" he exclaimed, with great anguish. Gabriel was riding shotgun, he was on the copilot's seat, and Junior was in the back. It was painfully obvious that, in coming to a complete stop, his seven-year-old son hit his face against the dashboard and cut himself in the process. He was not wearing a seatbelt. Most people, back then in Maracay, never wore seatbelts. Gabriel, upon his dad's reaction but unaware of his present state, was able to utter some words. The grammar was sufficiently coherent for Gilberto to realize that immediate emergency medical attention was not necessary. However, he was alarmed, agitated, enraged, outraged, and overtly excited at the sight of blood on his little boy's face as it trickled down his son's chubby milky-white cheeks. All this mishap because of an ignorant FOOL! Gilberto then turned his head to face forward and noticed that the FOOL did not even gesture to apologize or even acknowledge any wrongdoing. By this time, thick veins in Gilberto's forehead and neck enlarged and an endless sea of words started to unravel; only some of the language was discernible and rational. He subsequently turned back to face Gabriel again, only to aggravate his condition to an ultimate and inevitable climax. His eyes bulged out and adrenaline pumped through his body like *El Rio Orinoco*. He instinctively resolved to confront the other driver face to face. Without an ounce of hesitation, he opened the door and marched out, in rapid long strides, towards the culprit's car.

The FOOL apparently had his whole family in the car. The grandmother, the son, and the daughter rode in the back while the wife sat in the front. All the windows were closed. When Gilberto finally arrived, the FOOL, noticing the obvious intensity of Gilberto's demeanor opted to signal and talk through a tiny crack in the window, a deliberately small opening between the glass and the doorframe. Gilberto could no longer contain himself. He placed his fingers in the crack and pulled the window down two-thirds of the way. He then started swinging his fists left and

9

right! He threw the punches while simultaneously uttering derogatory words of disgust. It was an unbelievable scene of passionate distress! A parent's display of desperation! The boys, at this time, were still in the car and completely perplexed at the situation. The grandmother, in the meantime, yelled from within the cabin of the FOOl's car while everybody else from the same made sudden violent gestures. No one, however, exited the car. Driving off was not an option because they were still in the traffic gridlock.

After a minute or two of swinging away, Gilberto walked back to the Fairlane and, just at the time when he was about to sit in the car, he saw Gabriel's bloody cheeks again. A new burst of energy immediately drowned him for a second time. "WHAT? Do you want more? TELL ME! Is it that you want more? I WILL GIVE YOU MORE! *Pendejo!*" His body, itching from the rush of adrenaline, could not sustain itself and so it jumped.

As before, his fists and arms whipped back and forth through the window without showing any signs of fatigue. This time, in between punches, he stepped back and signaled the driver to step out and face him like a man. Before giving the driver a chance to react though, Gilberto closed the gap again and kept on swinging. This process continued for a couple of rounds. The driver never had a chance to get out of the car. This move might have been deliberate on Gilberto's part to ensure a painless victory. On the other hand, it might just have been the result of pure unadulterated exaltation and exasperation. Gilberto, eventually, walked back to his car. The driver, even in the interim of Gilberto's stroll to his car, did not attempt to get out of the car.

Not surprisingly, the episode repeated once more when Gilberto again saw the blood in Gabriel's face. "You want more! YOU IDIOT!" *Deja vu,* it was just like a broken record; the same scene repeated yet another time. Junior, from the backseat, finally came to his senses and realized, when looking within his own stained hands, that his brother's face was covered with *COLITA,* the red bloodlike dressing used to flavor the Raspado, and his dad mistakenly thought it was BLOOD! "Clean your face, Gabriel! Papy thinks you have *blood on your face!* CLEAN IT NOW!" By the time Gilberto came back, the traffic light was turning green and the cars, including that of the FOOL, started to drive off. "Papy, it is NOT BLOOD! It's Raspado. . . ."

We are, after all, the bright blinding headlights staring down Papy's eyes!

Bienvenue!

Green countryside, trees, remote warehouses, wide-open farms, electric poles, and train tracks were the images that passed before my eyes as my thoughts meandered aimlessly. I was tired and unable to sleep at the same time. The mere prospect of reaching *The City of Lights* consumed much of my thoughts. I had read much about *France's* grandiose beauty, magnificent culture, and astounding history. This trip, however, was my first visit and thus my first tangible exposure. I was a member of an adult volleyball team touring Western Europe. At present, we were on our way from *London* to *Paris.* Our plans were to play some volleyball against local clubs as well as to socialize with the teams and to visit some of the major tourist attractions.

French history, like many of the neighboring countries, is filled with picturesque tales of kings and queens, revolutions, and world-renowned artists dating back several centuries. As such, I was anxious to see the artwork inspired by such calamities as the persecution of the *Huguenots,* the storming of the *Bastille,* and the beheading of the unpopular *Marie Antoinette.* Of course, the paintings and the sculptures propelled by the church and by extravagant kings like the celebrated *Sun King,* King Louis XIV, also piqued my interest and enthusiasm. My partial knowledge of the language heightened the anticipation already built up to this point.

We finally arrived at the *Gare du Nord,* the train station. It was a cold November day! Cold dry air flowed in waves through the open station, thereby causing my muscles to tighten and my body to crunch in hopes of generating and conserving body heat.

Everybody was fully covered in layers of clothing, and many modeled furry winter hats as they briskly strolled about. At first, the sounds I heard from people's mouths only amounted to gibberish; but, little by little; they eventually became coherent sentences filled with meaningful expressions. I was amazed! My grammar and vocabulary was sufficiently preserved through the years to give me the power of understanding! I found myself speaking the language without apprehension within moments of my arrival. It really was not because I knew the language well; it was because I was not ashamed of my poor but, apparently, effective communicating skills. "*Quelle heure est-il?*" I asked a Frenchman to test his reaction to my pronunciation. He simply gave me the time and walked off, a good sign!

The locality was full of people walking in all directions, as would be expected from any major city. Some of us in the group had to get some *French francs* and thus waited a couple of minutes in our present position before departing. Upon commencing our walk, our coach told us that it wold take approximately fifteen minutes to get to the hotel. I cannot, with a clean conscience, attest to this estimate since all my senses feasted on the motley scenery presented by the strange yet, in someway, familiar city. The streets were narrow, and the height of the buildings did not surpass five or six floors. The sidewalks were filled with pedestrians of all ages; they walked at a rapid but uniform pace. The roar of cars, buses, and mopeds polluted the environment. Foreign voices and high-pitched horns adorned the colorful setting. The alternating aroma of gasoline, sweet perfumes, and fresh baked bread stimulated my sense of smell as we marched on the street and sidewalk.

It was not long until we found ourselves in the hotel. It was about half past four o'clock in the afternoon. The hotel was at the crossing of *Rue Montmartre* and *Rue Richer.* We agreed to go up to our rooms and get settled with the condition that we meet in the lobby half an hour later. The elevator was small and cramped, sized only for two full-sized or, perhaps, three medium-sized bodies. Three girls from our group crammed into the cabin and took the first ride. Taking note of the slowness of the elevator, I opted for the flight of stairs. The steps were narrow and the stairway was dark. The lighting all throughout the winding uphill trail was poor. Jeff, one of my teammates, and I shared a room on the fifth floor. The room was petite and, thankfully, had its own bathroom. A bathroom, as I had heard from stories back home, is a treasured commodity in Europe. Sharing one shower with the entire floor, I was told, is not uncommon. In any case, I put my bags in the room and, in anticipation of our awaited outing to the city, wasted no time in descending back down to the lobby. Needless to say, I was early and, as short as half an hour sounds, the wait seemed like an eternity to me.

Eventually, the rest of the group came down; at which point, our excursion commenced. We walked southbound on Rue Montmartre. Our coach was familiar with the city, and it was his intention to give us a customized guided tour. After a couple of blocks, we reached the entrance of the subway station. I thought our coach was merely pointing it out to us when I noticed that he, along with the group, descended into it. The words "Not Another Train!" quickly crossed my mind. I did not really feel like getting into the subway that offered very little with regards to views of the city. I therefore decided to break away from the group. Much to my surprise, I noticed that Irene, a fellow teammate, stood by me when I waved good-bye to the coach indicating that I would go on my own. *Great!* I thought. Irene is adventurous, self-assured, and, most of all, good company. She is also cognizant of big city life and very perceptive to its intricacies. So, upon looking at each other, we both said, almost simultaneously, "Oh, well!" and kept on walking.

We decided to walk towards the *Museé du Louvre,* which is on the north bank, north of *la Seine.* By walking south on Rue Montmartre, we were accomplishing our plan. The Louvre was a highlight that we did not want to miss, for it houses, among other works, *Venus de Milo* and Leonardo de Vinci's *Mona Lisa.* Its magnificent glass *Pyramide,* designed by architect I. M. Pei, at the entrance to the museum, is a well-conversed topic for its merits in architecture. It was also a source of considerable controversy ever since it was commissioned in 1983 to its final deployment in 1989. The time now was probably half past six o'clock in the evening, and my stomach started to growl a bit from hunger.

"How about some dinner?" I asked Irene to which she favorably agreed without hesitation. A few blocks farther, we found a restaurant called *Pied du Cochon,* French for pig's foot. An interesting name! I did not expect a restaurant with such a name to be in the middle of a city like Paris. The establishment, however, was quaint and ornate. Beautiful flowers decorated the entryway and all throughout the separate dining areas. The patrons wore expensive suits, black in color for the most part, and beautiful dresses, some short and others long. A highly trafficked and charming walkway bordered the restaurant.

By now, we were wondering if they would allow us inside. I was wearing a pair of black jeans with a thick brown leather jacket under which I wore a T-shirt. Irene was wearing a long-sleeve denim shirt with a black spandex bottom and a backpack. If there was a dress code, we certainly did not adhere to it! In any case, we were happy to see that we were not rejected. Dinner turned out to be a very enjoyable experience. We both started our meal with a delicious French Onion Soup. I, being on the adventurous side, had pig's foot as my main dish, *the specialty of the house.*It was quite tasty, but it had very little meat to it. The bone filled most of its mass. The skin was crunchy and the sauce was spicy. I do not remember what Irene had, but I recall that it looked good. We had red wine to accompany our meal and a delicious dessert to end it.

After the meal and a very gratifying conversation, we left the restaurant to re-embark on our adventure. In looking for a place to eat, we had deviated somewhat from our original course. We relied, however, on our sense of direction to continue our journey.

15

We walked and visually digested our immediate surroundings. Before long, the sky became quite dark, being probably somewhere around eight o'clock in the evening. We walked for a while until realizing that, if we were on the right path, we should have already been at our destination, the Louvre. This realization was not a source of concern since our purpose was to sightsee, be it what we knew to expect from the city or *what we did not know we, perchance, wanted to see.* The streets forked and curved. We turned right. We turned left. We went up some stairs and came back down again. Stores varied in nature, from selling cosmetics and articles of clothing to selling books and magazines.

The merchandise of the stores gradually changed from expensive thick furs to exotic thin lingerie. An adult-oriented store of the X-rated kind suddenly appeared. I took note of its appearance, but it did not necessarily surprise me. The streets went from being somewhat desolate of bodies and full of cars to being reasonably populated with pedestrians and extinct of cars. People seemed to congregate into groups at different corners. The density of X-rated stores unexpectedly grew to culminate in *one hundred percent.* Triple-X theatres and sex shops were now lined up right next to one another. Graffiti and sexy posters of women wearing small pieces of lingerie crowded the walls. The sidewalks and streets were now pretty dirty. The street we were on was covered in a plethora of soda cans, plastic cups, newspapers, rags, and broken bottles. The people were mostly dressed in obscure gloomy colors with overly worn jeans. Their hands were, for the most part, tucked into their jackets. Select and somewhat vociferous groups claimed ownership of particular corners on the street. Their hair was uncombed and unkempt. The lighting was dim, as though only emitted by yellow lights. Neon signs, of course, were imminent and ranging from fluorescent green and cherry red to electric blue.

Two prostitutes, and one of those in particular, caught my attention. It was her light clothing that struck me as unusual since, as I mentioned earlier, it had been cold that day! Her stature measured roughly five feet and six inches. A bright red silk dress gave a full view of her beautiful cleavage while concealing a double D-sized cup. The low-cut and strapped dress was bordered with black embroidery; it looked more like a nightgown than a dress. The thin smooth cloth could not camouflage the presence of a roll of soft skin protruding out of her waist side. The exposed skin of her shoulders, breast, thighs, and knees was milky white. The sleeves of a dark sweater hung from the ends of her shoulders while one hand busied itself with a burning cigarette, and the other rested on her shapely waist. She leaned against a wall, as if in a photographic pose, with a foot resting on the same, allowing her knee to bend ever so slightly. Her black hair was long and wavy. The thickness and density of her hair did not permit the wind to affect it much. Her eyes were pitch black, and her face was perfectly white with a soft smooth texture. Her features were symmetrical and showed no signs of scars whatsoever.

As we approached, I could see wrinkles at the ends of her eyes and at the edges of her mouth, where her round delicate cheeks rested. Her make-up was heavy but perfectly applied. Her dark red lips were thick; she was chewing gum at the time. She wore *rouge* on her cheeks. The skin of her neck creased as it stretched when she vigorously masticated. It was only the folds of her neck and the wrinkles of her face that divulged her age, a seemingly forty-year-old woman.

After passing her, we started noticing that the streets were inundated with black garbage bags, the ten-pound kind. They were open and full of clothing, particularly full of undergarments. "Strange!" This sight of Paris I did not envision. Irene and I commented on our ignorance of this part of the city and our fortune to have been exposed to it. Privileged, we thought, because we would have never seen this peculiar and unexpected part of town had we meticulously planned our outing. Immediately after, however, I started thinking about our safety and my ability to protect Irene and myself from any possible misfortune. I am sure Irene could protect herself, but I still felt responsible for her safety and well-being. I did not communicate these thoughts to her, though. Besides, except for the strange surroundings, no one had either approached us or talked to us. The population density lessened as we continued to walk. All of a sudden, we both noticed the consistent sound of footsteps behind us; someone walked in our wake, leaving five to ten yards of space in between. He had been walking at our pace, rather quick, and behind us for a block or two. This news alarmed us a bit. Both of us, having had experience in the city, showed no signs of distress. We stopped at a relatively populated corner, pretending to look at a storefront, to see the reaction of the prospective assailant. We noticed that he, too, stopped. He had a leather jacket similar to mine with his hands tucked into it. We only saw his profile and could barely distinguish any distinctive features since it was dark and our haste prevented us from taking a longer glance. We quickly decided to cross the street and continue walking.

He did not cross the street but began walking as soon as we started on the opposite side. Again, we stopped at the next corner to see his reaction. Much to our dismay, he stopped and lingered. I now noticed the loudness and quickness of the imminent palpitations within my chest. Did he want our money? Was he crazed with the intention of causing us harm? Did he have hidden companions waiting to prey on a couple of tourists like ourselves? All these questions flooded my thoughts in a matter of a second! We had to lose him but, somehow, we needed to keep our escape path along populated streets. This endeavor would prove to be difficult. Looking for help did not seem to be an option. The crowd we had seen, up to this point, was not the type to help. It is typical of situations like these that people ignore occurrences of the sort for their own safety. We thusly picked up our walking pace and turned right at the corner. Having some seconds to spare before he could catch another glimpse of us on the perpendicular street, our pace went from brisk to rapid. We made another turn. Suddenly, *I saw a light at the end of the tunnel!* I could see, at some distance, cars traversing through a lighted street. We headed like mad to that point! This stretch we did without looking back. Neither of us still showed signs of fear; instead, we were both resolute and confident, or so we thought our demeanor showed. *Never let a dog know you fear him!* Anyway, when we finally arrived at the lighted street, we turned around to see the state of our situation; he was gone! What a relief!

After quietly rejoicing for a minute or two, we continued our journey. There was no reason to cease sightseeing as long as we stayed on major inhabited streets. A block or two went by before we headed into a great big arch. Cars and buses drove through it. It was also illuminated but not with striking splendor. "Could this monument be the infamous *Arc de Triomphe?*" Somehow I pictured it more grandiose and ornate. However, being open minded and receptive to other possibilities, I spent a few minutes looking at it and resolved to take a couple of pictures. The pictures, by the way, never did come out. After the arch encounter, we pressed on. "Wait! Another one?" I exclaimed to Irene after a couple of blocks of walking. We stumbled onto another similar, if not exactly equal, arch. "It cannot be! Did we walk in a circle? No!" These arches, obviously, were not what I had thought. I guess the Arc de Triomphe is not the only arch in Paris.

Still with the Louvre in mind, we pushed onwards. In what seemed like less than a minute, we suddenly found ourselves in the middle of a loud vociferous rally, a protest of sorts! The rapid haste ignited caution in our actions. My fear was that this kind of manifestation, in the part of town we apparently resided, could invite violence. However, after the relative triumph of our most recent experience, we felt sufficiently secure to step aside for a moment and simply watch. Apparently, African residents complained about some immigration policy. Large picket signs were held high and hands were waved abruptly in every direction. Loud low-pitched voices under a deep muffled roar permeated throughout the immediate surroundings. People yelled and marched chaotically while the sounds of drums kept a rhythmic and persistent beat. Their behavior showed evidence of belligerence. Embedded in the crowd, a couple of cars resided. I do not know if these automobiles belonged to the protestors or if they were inadvertently caught in the middle of it. "What turn of events!" We went from a desolate dark street to a full-grown and fully lit, possibly dangerous rally!

Eventually, we found our way to the Louvre! The building structure spanned one or two full-sized blocks, a vast coverage! Numerous, brightly illuminated statues lined up the walls of the complex. The Pyramide proved to be gorgeous and quite amazing. It was half-past nine o'clock in the evening, at this point. We did not expect to find the museum open, of course. It was open, though! As it turns out, they close late on Wednesdays, a quarter before ten o'clock.

We had a chance to walk inside through the beautiful Pyramide, what a sight! Being late, we wasted little time in studying the layout of the museum and proceeded to simply find the salon where the *Mona Lisa* was housed. We entered, and to our surprise, we were not charged to get in nor did we take time to ask. We might have entered through the exit illegally, but we had too little time to think about it and thusly proceeded to go inside without delay. Beautiful paintings, breathtaking sculptures, and mind-boggling ceilings astonished us beyond belief. Words cannot give justice to the magnificence of the artwork. As we walked through the museum, sighs of amazement drowned our voices. It was not long before we were escorted out, though. Closing time had arrived.

From a quiet delightful dinner in a romantic backdrop to a colorful and dangerous journey through some of the dark forgotten streets to a beautiful mind-boggling museum on center stage paint a revealing portrait of the many faces of Paris, *a textured yet smooth palette of vivid colors!*

A Christmas Tale

You have the right to remain silent. Anything you say can and will be used against you in a court of law. You have the right to consult an attorney before questioning. You have the right to have your attorney present with you at all times during questioning. If you cannot afford an attorney, one will be appointed for you at no expense to you. You may choose to exercise these rights at any time. Do you understand your rights?

I do.

You are being charged with aggravated assault of one Robertino Weatherthorpe. . . .

That is when my mind started wandering and I stopped listening. I have heard the *Miranda Rights* on television before, but I never imagined in a million years that they would be recited to *ME!* The policeman mumbled some more, but the words didn't make any sense to me anymore. As he spoke, he wrapped my hands around my back and placed them in a pair of cold metallic handcuffs. I could feel my wrist bones crushed against the hard alloy! The officer then proceeded to shove and push me toward the police car. I stared at the ground while stumbling over to the car; I only raised my eyes occasionally and in a half daze. God! I couldn't think or see clearly. The journey felt like it lasted for hours. I could barely keep my balance. the officer held the handcuffs so high and out that my arms felt as though they were being pulled out of their sockets. A thousand and one images flashed in front of my eyes. I saw myself in a tiny stinky jail cell with a small stained toilet and a thin white pad for a mattress. I could envision Dad sitting on the sidewalk with his elbows rested against his knees and his hands holding his head. Mom, well, she was cooking brunch in the kitchen, a meal we had last Saturday around two o'clock in the afternoon.

Come on! Duck and get into the car. Don't resist!

I wasn't really trying to offer any resistance. It is just that I felt disoriented and could not really walk straight. The stocky officer pushed me inside the back cabin of the car and shut the door behind me. The seats were black and made of vinyl. The cabin was spotless with a freakish new car smell. A couple of ambulances were still on the crime scene, and so were five other police cars. A curious crowd gazed motionless from a distance, all of them were lined up outside the police tape and around the parking lot. There was a bright light, next to a big bushy tree and in front of the ambulance, just outside of the police barricade. In front of it, a lady in a light blue blouse and a short black skirt spoke into a microphone. I must have made the news!

Anyway, another officer got into the car and cranked the engine. I could tell that the red and blue lights stopped flashing. That is when the car suddenly jolted and we started moving.

Oh, God, what have I done?

*　　*　　*

It started by the cheese stand in the supermarket. People were all over the place. Everyone was in a hurry, like they usually are every major holiday. The aisles were crammed and the deli line was long. All the carts were taken and most of the hand baskets were gone. It was like rush hour in New York City, except cars had taken the shape of carts. It was a typical December 24, I guess. People always get ready for a big holiday by buying lots of food! Like it happens so many times in the big cities, unfortunately, the spirit of the season seems to be washed away by the stress of last-minute shopping. Most of the joy was sucked out of people's faces! The lines leading into the cash registers were so long that people could not even cross from aisle to aisle and could barely get to some select food items. Mom and I went around the crowd, by the side, and started walking our way through the dairy aisle.

At the end of the aisle, when we were crossing over to the next aisle, a fat balding man decided to insult Mom. I didn't expect it at all. I was across the cheese stand from the man when I heard his remarks. Keeping my cool and the spirit of the season in mind, I rushed around to confront the man and, without screaming or swinging any punches, I simply demanded respect.

Don't talk to my mother that way. RESPECT HER. THERE IS NO REASON FOR INSULTS AND I WON'T TOLERATE THEM!

I stood so close to him that our noses were within an inch of each other. My fists were clenched out of rage. My eyes were fixated on his. I could not really see what his hands were doing. The traffic around us ceased moving, of course. That is when I felt three fingers on my face, around my right eye. He scratched, while pushing me back. It totally caught me by surprise. Hell broke loose then! I started swinging and punched him in the stomach. Mom yelled and walked toward the fight in an attempt to stop it. All of a sudden, while winding for another punch, I heard a loud screech and Mom fell to the floor. I stood still for a second, turned around, and quickly kneeled by her when I realized what happened.

MOMMMM!!!!!

Her face was turning tomato red. Her ears were burning up, and her eyes were glassy and half-closed. Dad and I have seen these symptoms before; they were usually the result of hypertensive attacks. The doctor had warned us that any more episodes like these could be fatal or quite damaging. They could trigger a stroke, which might leave Mom dead or paralyzed. I PANICKED! I was not ready to lose Mom like this. She was crying all the while when, all of a sudden, she stopped and closed her eyes. Her face leaned over to the side with her mouth still open and her arms dropped like dumbbells.

OH, MY GOD!!! GOD!!!

I stopped thinking. I stopped feeling. I stopped living. I got off my knees and ran wildly toward the stupid balding man. I could only see one thing: a big fat moronic idiot. My fists were launched, and punches were thrown left and right. I could not feel any of my limbs. It was like in a bad dream. I dished out numerous punches, and I think only half of them actually connected. The other half went into thin air, and a few of them even landed on the stands where groceries once stood. A good number of the blows, though, landed square on his belly. He, too, started swinging and fighting back.

Not too long after my initial attack, we were both on the ground. I was sitting on his belly and swinging at his face from side to side, one cheek at a time. Blood not only gushed out of his upper lip and underneath his right eyebrow but also from my face and fiery fists. My knuckles were bleeding and impressions of his teeth were permanently imprinted on them. I couldn't feel any pain, though. I couldn't hear anything. I couldn't even see anything around me. The world shrunk into a single spot and time wrapped itself in a loop round one instant. The rage was so intense that no one dared get in between the punches. With every punch, I expelled a loud grunt.

He eventually gained enough energy to roll over and push me over to the side. As he started getting up, I wound up from the floor and shot my fist right to his face with all my might. My hand came up and down until it landed on his right cheek. His head whipped back and bounced on the ground a couple of times as he fell back to the floor. "THUMP, THUMP." I jumped on top of him again and started darting a few more punches. It was a couple of blows into it when I realized that he was unconscious. I stopped swinging and sat frozen.

There was blood all over the floor, his and mine. My T-shirt was ripped and also drenched in blood, not to mention sweat. My hands were numb and my knees ached. A couple of seconds passed, and someone pulled me off. As he tried to raise me, though, I flung my arms free, got up, and ran through the aisle toward Mom. She was lying flat on the floor. The store manager and two attendants were sitting beside her. They were flapping a couple of magazines back and forth to give her some air. Then, I heard police sirens.

MOVE!!!!! LET ME GET TO MOM! SOMEONE CALL THE PARAMEDICS! PLEASE!!!!

They're already on their way! someone, from within the crowd, answered.

People didn't hesitate to let me through. Mom lay there motionless. Even though she was unconscious, her expression was rigid and harsh. Stress and pain was impressed on her eyes, temples, and forehead. I didn't know what to think. My chest was about to explode. My heart was pounding fast and loud. My eyes stung and started to water uncontrollably. The image of her head leaning on a bag of rice and her arms resting lifeless on her delicate stomach was too much for me. I wrapped my arms around her, placed my head on her stomach, and wept.

A good half-hour must have passed before I felt four hands pull me up. They grabbed me hard and yanked me with commanding force. It was the police. Immediately after, the paramedics came and put Mom on a stretcher. They wheeled her out of the supermarket. Another stretcher also rolled out behind hers.

Did you fight that gentleman on the stretcher? the cop asked.

Yes, I fought that son of a bitch!

Well, you are going to jail for that so-called SON OF A BITCH! Come on!

* * *

How is Mom?

25

Son, your mom is in ICU right now. She is in a coma.

God! The day had started out so well and now. . . . I can't believe she is in a freaking coma. I can't believe I'm in jail! And who knows for how long! DAMN IT! DAMN IT! My world is crumbling. My world is dead.

Gabrielito, tell me. What happened? Why the fight? Why?

Well, Dad, it was because of a stupid cart. We had a small basket and needed a cart to carry all the groceries we expected to buy. All the carts were taken, unfortunately. Then, we saw an unattended cart by the milk section with one item on it. Mom traded it for her basket. The owner turned out to be this retarded Robertino character. He appeared about a minute later and was quite belligerent! In a harsh and patronizing tone, he demanded his cart back. Who would actually comply with a bully like that! Mom and I refused to give it and pressed on with our shopping. We walked one more aisle when we met up again with the guy, and that is when he started with the name-calling. He insulted Mom, not me. I guess he felt more comfortable picking on a woman. I confronted him, of course, which ultimately led to our fight and my eventual defeat.

You mean to tell me this is all because of a stupid cart? Your mom may die and you may have sacrificed YOUR life, your career, for a cart? For an unstable idiot who didn't have anything better to do than to fight a mother and her son?

On the Road Again!

Four friends representing a world-renowned company from the "Lone Star State" found themselves traveling together to a highly respected technical conference in San Francisco. It was in the dead of winter of 1999, the middle of February. The conference is held annually, typically lasting five days. This one started on Sunday with tutorials and ended on Thursday with a short course. The primary objective of the conference was to present state-of-the-art discoveries to the general engineering community. Papers were presented all day Monday, Tuesday, and Wednesday. Panel discussions were arranged for two of the five evenings. The travelers, Mike, Bob, Gabe, and Wei, took advantage of the free times in-between sessions, though, to visit the beautiful sites of San Francisco.

Mike, Wei, and Bob were all married. The former two already had children roaming at home, and the latter had one on the way. Gabe was the bachelor of the group. They were all prominent professionals, holding post-graduate degrees, Master's and Ph.D's, in the field of electrical engineering.

Anyway, the foursome had Sunday afternoon and evening free to wander around the city and perhaps visit some of the sites beyond the city limits. They chose to visit Muir Woods, north of Golden Gate Bridge. The drive took approximately half an hour to an hour from Fisherman's Wharf. The visit was refreshing! The site was adorned with majestic trees aging several hundreds of years. The weather was very humid and the scenery quite green. A creek pierced the mountain through the motley wooded site. Relaxing wounds of water running through rocks and around trees permeated the environment. It was cold! The thick and tall trees filtered the sunlight but not the wind; at least that was how it felt. After seeing and experiencing enough of this natural wonder, Bob suggested that we should perhaps visit Mount Tam, short for Mount Tamalpais, a tall mountain about another half an hour away from Muir Woods. It overlooks the bay and the Pacific Ocean with a great view of Alcatraz. The like-minded group agreed immediately and without hesitation. By now, the time was about thirty minutes past five o'clock in the evening.

The roads leading to the mountain were great! They winded up and about the mountain. Every corner was filled with picturesque views of the mountain, the bay, or the ocean. Bob, the designated driver, kept alluding to a short drive to the entrance of the park housing the peak of the mountain. Bob had already made this excursion several years ago. The drive, however, actually seemed a little longer than what Bob's impression seemed to suggest. No one in the group seemed to mind the wait, though. The stunning scenery was sufficient to more than satisfy and even entertain the passengers.

The entry gate to the park was finally reached. At this point, it was a quarter past six o'clock. Unfortunately, a sign posted on the entry read "Park closes at 6:00 P.M" a bummer! The park apparently closed fifteen minutes prior to their arrival. A metal bar interrupted the inward traffic; however, the outbound traffic did not have any such obstacle. "*LET'S DRIVE IN THROUGH THE EXIT!* What is the worst that could happen anyway?" Gabe said animatedly.

"Yeah! Let's do it!" Bob replied with equal enthusiasm and vigor. Mike and Wei both agreed. Of course, the gate was not manned nor was there a ranger overlooking the entry. Bob said the drive should be short and quick. The winding roads past the gate illustrated even more beautiful scenery than before. The turns were tight enough to warrant speeds of under fifteen miles per hour.

Sounds that are characteristic to raw nature were loud and omnipresent. Several cars were driving in the opposite direction, down the mountain, to no surprise to the group since the park was closed. After several minutes of driving through the road, another gate was encountered. This gate had the same sign, but the entry was not blocked. The group kept driving up!

Finally, after passing yet another sign indicating that the park was closed, the top was reached. The small parking lot led to a walking trail, which supposedly led to the peak of the mountain. Some people were walking out of the trail and into their cars. At this time, the sun was setting. Disregarding yet another sign, the group decided to continue onward and follow the trail. "After all this, let's go all the way!" The trail, at first, was outlined with pieces of wood. However, this ended soon thereafter. The trail became narrow, crooked, and filled with rocks and stones. Preventing an ankle sprain was a chore, even with the light emitted by the sunset.

To no one's surprise, Bob said: "It is only a short walk, we should reach the top in no time!" Well, needless to say, it was not a short trail, but the group found the scenery and the adventure sufficiently stimulating to prevent them regretting the ride. Mike eventually reached a point where he decided to stop, enjoy the view, and go back the trail. The others, however, were not so inclined and therefore pressed on. About twenty yards farther, Gabe thought he had reached the peak and Bob confirmed it. They both yelled out: "Mike: come another twenty yards, we've reached the top!" Less than forty seconds passed when they realized that they had not finished the trail. Mike, upon arriving to the misidentified peak, decided to stop and go back. The group, except for Mike, continued to walk up the trail.

Bob, Gabe, and Wei reached the top soon after. The sun was already asleep by now. The view was amazing though! Wei enthusiastically proclaimed: "*THIS IS BREATHTAKING!*" All three shared the sentiment. Less than a minute passed before, out of the blue, a voice emerged out of the dark and lonely night.

It said: "Would the driver and passengers of a red rental car please come back to their car immediately. *THE PARK IS CLOSED!*" Gabe, Bob, and Wei looked at each other with amazement and perplexing expressions!

"We are in trouble!" someone said. "We might as well finish by taking another minute or two to watch the rest of the scenery though!" a compatriot exclaimed. "Yeah! Let's see the rest of it since we have already committed the infraction!" the last one agreed.

All this from the mouths of highly educated engineers on the verge of perhaps being taken to jail! After taking a good look, the bandits finally decided they should head back. After several yards, all of a sudden, they realized that they were not on the trail. This realization did not surprise them since it was pitch dark; nevertheless, it did startle them. "This is not the trail!" Wei said with a hint of agitation.

"This way!" Bob replied reassuringly. After another few steps, they realized again that their newly found path also led them astray! How could they expect to find a trail in the darkness of night, especially one that did not resemble much like a trail! Another possible route was found that somehow looked, or perhaps felt, more familiar than the others did. Since the available choices were limited and they had already concluded that the other two possible paths were not the right ones, they pursued this last option. The presumed trail continued and more familiar turns were found. This looked like the right trail after all!

The lack of light and the abundance of stones and rocks made the trail very dangerous. Arms and hands had to be extended outward to partially feel the way through the rocks as well as to provide leverage and balance. The temperate dropped and only the sounds of the wind, as it penetrated the leaves of surrounding trees, and the sound of moving rocks, as they were inadvertently kicked off the feet, could be heard. A few jokes along the way seemed to relax the group a bit, but the danger of tripping and falling was prevalent and in everybody's minds. The topic of snakes also came up! This fear-prone topic was quickly dismissed to alleviate tension.

Suddenly, the voice of the ranger again polluted the environment: "Would the driver. . . ." The group, of course, knew they were in trouble, not only because of their present physical predicament but also because of the awaited punishment. "Didn't Mike reassure the ranger that we were probably on our way back down?" someone commented.

The march through the crooked and narrow trail persisted. Finally, the part of the trail that was outlined in wood was encountered! Depth perception, however, was limited and the stairs were not discernible to the naked eye. Visual impairment was compensated with small, though rapid, strides. A light source was finally identified far into the distance. The emitted light was that of light post illuminating the parking lot located at the foot of the trail where the final warning of a closed park resided. Two cars became distinguishable, the familiar red Pontiac and a truck with roof lights. A somewhat heavyset gentleman with a jacket stood by the truck with a note pad. Mike was leaning against the truck with his hands in the pockets of long black winter coat.

As Wei, Gabe, and Bob approached the parking lot, the ranger turned towards the group and began by saying: "Hello, gentlemen. You have committed two major violations! You entered a closed area despite repeated warnings against doing so; at least four warning signs were posted. Furthermore, you also neglected to pay the entry fee to the park. The . . ." The group stood quiet and attentive throughout the long sermon awaiting the inevitable conclusion, the punishment! ". . . had it taken a few more minutes for you to come back down, I would have had to call in for rescue," the ranger continued. "The way I see it, you have one of two choices:

you can either send the money for the ticket I am giving you through mail or you can let the rental car agency take care of it."

A sigh of relief was felt when the bandits heard this last statement! The punishment was only a ticket! What is even more astonishing is that the rental car agency seemed to be liable and not the group, a bit unfair for the agency. As the ranger drove off, Gabe said: "*LET THE AGENCY TAKE CARE OF IT!* I think it is only a parking ticket. In any case, they will bill us if they see fit."

Bob, a little nervous and shaken, replied: "Sure! However, if I get billed, I will bill you guys for an even cut!" The car was under his name after all.

After a second or two, when they started to open the doors to get into the car, Wei said: "Mike, you missed a *BREATHTAKING VIEW!*"

Gabe, on the same humorous note, supported this sentiment with: "If you had only kept going a few more yards, what a shame!" The adventure ended as they headed down the mountain towards Golden Gate Bridge culminating the evening with dinner at Fisherman's Wharf.

Who said children ever grow up?

Baptism into the Brotherhood!

In the hopes of meeting girls, as was always the case, David and Jorge prepared themselves for a night in the town. The year was nineteen hundred and eighty-five. The young brothers' plan was to meet a few friends and to go to the local teenage discothèque, *Randolf's*, to hang out and to meet girls. David, the younger of the two, was thirteen years old while Jorge was seventeen. Despite the age difference, which teenagers usually perceive to be extreme, they were great buddies and loyal companions.

The brothers were originally from Venezuela and had only lived in *North Miami Beach* not more than two or three years. Their interests revolved around sports and women. They were athletes and both played for their school, *Lear School's* Junior and Senior High School teams, respectively. Their circle of friends surpassed the boundaries of race and ranged from *red-blooded Americans* and *die-hard Argentineans* to *proud Cubans* and *vociferous Puerto Ricans*. Some of them were dedicated athletes, others were carefree classmates, and others were party buddies. Nearly all their friends were in Jorge's age group. Consequently, David had the privilege of maturing at a relatively fast rate.

Going to dance clubs was one of their favorite pastimes, especially for David. All the girls were older than he was, and none of them really objected to *cutting the rug* with him. His young inoffensive persona actually allowed him to dance intimately close to the girls, so close that not even a ray of light could squeeze between the tightly unified and melded bodies. The seemingly young David thusly enjoyed the full breadth of the warm soft figures of many sixteen- and seventeen-year-old girls. Jorge, on the other hand, would meet the girls and talk to them, but they would not so easily permit him to have full tangible appreciation of their bodies.

As the particular night progressed, David and Jorge went to meet Byron at his mom's apartment. Byron, a fellow soccer player, was an avid dancer, a smooth talker, and a reliable friend. Upon getting ready, Byron drove the group to the predetermined dance club of choice, Randolf's. The car was a long bright yellow LTD station wagon. It, being owned by a music enthusiast, had a spectacular stereo system equipped with a couple of twelve-inch woofers along with a pair of tweeters and mid-range speakers in the rear, a high-quality equalizer, and an insanely powerful amplifier. The system required so much electric power that a dual battery system had to be installed. In fact, the radio could only operate when the engine was running; the battery would quickly drain otherwise. The distinctiveness of the car was already well known among the teenage crowd and easily recognizable, by its unique looks but mostly by its almost supernatural ability to carry tunes, from a distance of at least a couple of hundred yards.

It was roughly nine o'clock when they arrived at their destination. Randolf's was located in *Poehman's Plaza* near 183rd Street and Biscayne Boulevard. The strip shopping mall consisted of several stores. The arrangement of the stores and the walkways was not symmetrical nor were they regular in nature. The layout had the feel of a concrete urban park with metal benches, palm trees, and assorted plants scattered throughout the decorated grounds. Despite the façade, the structural design was simple and not very impressive. All the stores, except for three, closed by six or seven o'clock in the evening. The establishments that remained open through the night until the early hours of the following morning were Randolf's, naturally, a video arcade, and an eight-theatre movie complex. A teenager's paradise!

That night, the mall was stormed with people. The threesome parked in their usual space, two to three rows from the dance club.

They met casual acquaintances there, people with whom they had visited during other similar outings. They hung out, as they initially always do, at the entrance of the club where the bouncers and other enthusiasts resided. The purpose was to check out the action while, at the same time, trading stories and telling insignificant lies. The perspective from the door gave a full view of the joint without the penalty of price. Ascertaining possible prospects, girls, was easily achieved from that angle! It was generally a good location to meet people since they all had to traverse through this point, the only available entrance. Additionally the entire assembly of cool and respected personalities usually congregated here.

The loud sounds projected from inside the club could probably be heard a mile away. Talking in such an environment required good vocal strength and stamina. It was typical to lose one's voice in less than three hours. This constraint, however, did not stop the multitude from joking, laughing, yelling, pushing, and amusing themselves. The odor inherent to the locality was typical of such places. The sweet smell of perfume mixed with the manly odor of cologne and clashed with the *sophisticated stench* of burned cigarettes and the *proverbial reek* of sweat derived from danced-out bodies. The smoky cloud that floated throughout the club, as a result, penetrated deep into the eyes of many. It flowed in raging waves causing the eyes to twitch and to burn until eventually becoming bloodshot.

The popularity of the mall surpassed city limits and attracted teenagers from *South Beach, Fort Lauderdale, Hialeah, North Miami, South Miami,* and the "*Sowesera,*" Miami's southwest. Many of the attendees did not even enter the club, the movies, or the arcade. They just used the mall to "hang out" and show off. Others did not even get out of their cars. They would just drive by the club repeatedly, one after the other, proudly parading their cars. Some of the vehicles had air shocks that allowed them to bounce up and down with great dexterity while others had powerful engines that generated loud low-pitched roaring sounds. Many of the riders stuck their heads out to attract attention. The place stank of testosterone! The constant yet slow flow of cars lasted for hours on end.

Sometime after eleven or twelve o'clock, Jorge went to the car to look for something. David, of course, followed. Upon their return, as they were walking across the parking lot by the club, a black 1978 firebird with dark-tinted windows aggressively and abruptly stopped an inch or less away from the brothers' legs. The sound of the music coming out of the hermetically sealed vehicle seemed to overwhelm the club's. The monster machine even rattled and vibrated in response to the rhythmic muffled sounds generated from the stereo within. When the brothers turned to face the car, they noticed that its passengers filled all possible cabin space.

They were several large black males. They waved their hands furiously while cursing to their hearts' content. Apparently, they were negatively predisposed to the brothers, a seemingly inoffensive and vulnerable pair. Thick drops of hot sweat ran down the brothers' faces while their legs kept trying to maintain some sense of balance. They, being of sound mind though, decided to refrain from making any sudden movements and to continue their journey to the sidewalk, to a less precarious area.

Much to the brothers' surprise, the crowd at the entrance of the club, with whom the brothers had conversed earlier, reacted to the belligerent attack of the black car. As it turned out, these guys were members of a White-American/Hispanic gang. The barely acquainted gang members jumped to the aid of the brothers. They surrounded the car from all sides except from the front and urged the driver and his passengers to "TAKE A HIKE!" while vigorously shaking the car from side to side. The passengers took out a wooden bat and waved it but only from within the car. All the while, they articulated: "WE'LL BE BACK MOTHER F——ERS! COUNT ON IT!" Soon after, the car accelerated, peeling out the tires, and ultimately disappeared into the dead of night.

The brothers were shaken but showed, in spite of it all, a casual and debonair demeanor. They felt somewhat at ease because their company was not dangerous to THEM, a good gang as far as they were concerned. They realized that these friendly hooligans had reacted perhaps not to defend a couple of nobodies from South America but to attack a sworn enemy. However, this conjecture was speculative and irrelevant at the time. Afterwards, the group, as a whole, took the threat lightly despite of its fearful intent. The general thought was: "They are too afraid to come back! Those sons of bitches!" *Dogs that bark don't bite!* The overall ambiance slowly relaxed to its normal joyous yet highly volatile state. Cars continued to roll, and a sense of coolness and triumph drowned all the commotion. Jorge and David never literally entered the club and eventually opted to see a movie instead. The theatre was down a corner and about thirty to forty yards away from the club. Another equally large pack of people waited patiently in line to buy tickets, four files extending back approximately fifteen to twenty yards.

While the brothers looked at the colorful movie posters, all of a sudden, several cars stopped in front of the movie theatre about forty yards away. The riders got out with bats and other miscellaneous objects. Their conduct did not inspire safety! Their movements were quite abrupt and drastic. They waved to each other as if signaling to charge and to attack. As they approached the theatre, their *gladiator faces,* tight with rage, voiced soft growls. The brothers, realizing their imminent danger, ran back to the club to seek a secure haven while warning the others of the frightful events to come. The good gang took this gesture to be altruistic and a true symbol of loyalty. They figured that it was a warning for the gang's sake and not for the brothers' selfish agenda. The group consequently sprinted like wild stallions to the theatre where the black mob rapidly converged from another angle. Toto, a friendly hooligan whose real name was Antonio, took one of the metal poles from the lines leading into the box office as a weapon.

Soon after, the others dismantled the rest of the poles and

similarly armed themselves. The crowd quickly disassembled and took flight. A good portion of the spectators, though, did not have a chance to get away from the scene and thus resolved to disperse towards the surrounding walls, away from the action. Many of them were yelling and screaming. *It was something right out of a movie!* Shirts were ripped and jeans were torn. Blood flew like spit as fists and bats made contact with tender flesh. Some guys, while on the floor, were violently kicked, pushed, and tossed. The all-out wrestling match was intensive, and there was no way of ascertaining the potential victors of the encounter. It was impressive to see Vince, from the friendly gang, handle two huge muscle-bound brutes. He was about five feet eleven inches and built like a football player. By this time, his shirt was off and stains of blood trickled over his face and his upper body, whether the blood belonged to him or not was impossible to establish.

Jorge and David, being curious and somewhat involved, ended at the edge of the audience bordering the *Roman Colisseo*. Jorge, showing signs of agitation and outrage, tripped a couple of the opposing gang members who happened to cross in front; they were wrestling others at the time. David, taking this reaction to be the preamble of his brother's intention to fight, whispered with force and passion: "*Que haces?* Don't fight, Hermano! Let's leave!" He exclaimed these words while holding Jorge's long-sleeve shirt and simultaneously fixating his eyes on the vicious battle. Jorge, without hesitation, turned and answered: "*No te preocupes,* I am not going to fight! I am faking it!" This response, coupled with a familiar stare, which was an effective form of communication for the pair, made David understand. It was the opportunity to show, or rather to fake, that they too fought side by side with the good gang. The fact that the encounter had initiated as a result of the brothers served to inspire them. Acknowledging Jorge's response, however, did not really mitigate the anguish of the experience nor did it pacify the emotional intensity. David resolved to support his brother wholeheartedly.

From the edge of the crowd, they both stuck out their feet and their fists, waving them like madmen. They made these gestures only when the friendly gang took notice and when it was relatively safe. They made sure that the black gangsters did not confuse them to be part of the fighting forces. Quite suddenly, the sounds of police sirens silently but distinctly permeated the place from a distance. Their volume grew rapidly. Many of the warriors took the opportunity to run. Some of the main players, though, fought to the very end. The cops finally arrived. The grounds were suddenly flooded with policemen. They jumped and slapped handcuffs left and right. They pulled the seeming untamable gladiators apart and threw them against the wall with brutal force and determination. Their reaction matched the intensity of the situation. Some of the bloodstained bodies were dragged back to the police cars while others, still resisting, were vehemently escorted.

The brothers, at the sight of the cops, quickly blended deep into the crowd and slowly stepped away from the scene. They were quite relieved to see the cops take action. After witnessing the apprehension of the unlucky few, the brothers spotted, in the distance, a few of the friendly hooligans who escaped the vicious hands of the police. Toto, the fearless Puerto Rican, was part of the group. As the brothers walked in their general direction, Toto signaled and invited them over. With the demeanor of trusted lifelong partners, the whole group, including the brothers, commented on the events claiming triumph and crediting it to unity. The rush of adrenaline was still high. *Jorge's plan apparently worked!* The gang actually thought the brothers fought! This conclusion, of course, was supported by the vivid recollection the brothers told the group, a somewhat embellished account. The gang had obviously accepted the brothers into their circle. Although the brothers were not official gang members, the group pledged, in actions and not in so many words, allegiance and eternal protection. *What turn of events!* What started out as being a search for girls ended up being the unofficial initiation into a gang! It was this night's chain of events that baptized the young brothers into the brotherhood!

The prospect of hanging out with the group, however, was not attractive to the brothers. *A game of fists is the game of VILLAINS!* Real and raw danger was not as inviting and entertaining as the company of pretty girls. The brothers, nevertheless, acknowledged the fraternity of which they now became virtual members and exclaimed their necessary casual hellos upon unplanned but inevitable encounters.

An Olympic Adventure!

It was the summer of 1996, and as luck would have it, I was living in Atlanta, Georgia, the home of the *1996 Summer Olympic Games.* The city dressed itself, like never before, for the gala event. *Downtown, Underground, Georgia State University, Georgia Tech (Georgia Institute of Technology)*, the *Olympic Stadium* (now called *Turner Field*), and other sites had the distinct privilege of officially hosting the games. In downtown, *Peachtree Street,* which runs predominately in the north-to-south direction, was closed and fully dedicated for pedestrian traffic. Only official vehicles for security and emergency purposes were allowed in this area. *International Boulevard,* also off-limit to cars, led the crowd from Peachtree Street down to *Centennial Olympic Park,* a playground built specifically, as the name implies, for the event at hand. Businesses, mainly retail and entertainment, also readied themselves for the feeding frenzy! Stores stocked up their inventory and allocated resources to actively promote themselves for the Olympic opportunity. Parking garages expected to make a "killing!" Other non-retail related business located in the heart of downtown, however, took a different approach. For the most part, they took a two-week vacation. Others accommodated their employees with telecommuting services, thereby allowing them to work from home and to interact with each other via modem-like telephone connections.

When the games started, I went to celebrate with the raucous yet sympathetic crowd almost on a daily basis. The streets were filled with visitors from all over the world! Japan, Mexico, Australia, France, Italy, Sweden, Venezuela, Argentina, Canada, England, Brazil, and other countries around the globe were well represented. They populated the streets beyond their physical capacity. International Boulevard, appropriately named, was so heavily dense with bodies that, when swerving through the mob, one could not help bumping into other folks each step of the way. There were several large concert stages and a variety of festival sites lasting all day and throughout the two weeks the party was held. Underground had one concert stage and Centennial Olympic Park had at least two others, not to mention yet another off of International Boulevard. *Hard Rock Café* and *Planet Hollywood,* located at the crossing of International Boulevard and Peachtree Street, were immensely popular. Jazz, Rock, Pop, Alternative, Classical, Blues, Country, Romantic, Rhythm and Blues, Mexican, Caribbean, and Reggae were but a few of the many different styles and flavors of music that were heard throughout the city. Men, women, and children were mostly in shorts and thin tank tops. Many of the guys had their T-shirts hanging down from their heads to protect their necks and faces from getting sunburned. In doing so, the chest, stomach, and back were bare to feel whatever breeze was available. Cowboy hats, baseball caps, and stylish beer-holding caps were popular items. Folks paraded around with portable battery-powered, hand-held fans and water misters.

On Friday July 26, as I had done on previous days, I went downtown again to enjoy the games and participate in the celebration. I dedicated the whole day for this activity. I parked at the crossing of Fourteenth Street and I-75. I walked from that point to downtown, which is a good long hike. At around eight o'clock in the evening, I was still enjoying myself. I was, at that time, in Underground, drinking a cool refreshing glass of Coke, an expensive commodity. I then decided to stroll down to Centennial Olympic Park to join in the main festivities held there. It was dark and people were still over the place. Many of them were deeply tanned, as I was, from the consistent daylong exposure to the hot summer sun. We were also drenched in sticky sweat, a consequence of the customary high humidity that Atlanta is well known to have in the middle of summer. The music was blaring from the concert stage, and I was beginning to feel tired. I looked for a bench near the stage to park my body for a while. My muscles were cramping a little from all the walking and the standing. Once seated, I found an electric pole nearby and reclined against it while watching and breathing in everything the environment around me had to offer.

The time now was about one in the morning, and I was still sitting. I was saving energy to stand up and march all the way back to my car, which had proven, in the past few days, to take more than thirty-five to forty-five minutes to walk to. Quite suddenly, about twenty minutes past one in the morning, *A LOUD AND POWERFUL BLAST* reverberated throughout the much-celebrated park. The thundering sound made the ground tremble. Subsequently, my hearing became impaired. Silent images and flashes of people under various lighting conditions quickly filled my tunneled vision as if in slow motion. The periphery surrounding these images was blurry and fuzzy. Time had slowed down, and I was viewing it one frame at a time! "OH, MY GOD!" "JESUS!" "MON DIEU!" "OH, LORD!" "AHHHHH!" "DIOS!" Almost immediately after, I felt a momentary sharp pain in my leg. The crowd went wild. A peculiar odor permeated the park, like the smell of fireworks during the celebration of July Fourth. The aura of joyous excitement had turned chaotic. Men and women of all ages and races ran almost aimlessly in all directions. Many of them dove to the ground, trying to seek cover under the benches throughout the park, under concession stands, and behind street poles.

Upon trying to get off my bench, my right leg felt numb and it could barely support my weight. Consequently, I opted to drop to the ground and roll under the bench. "Could this be a robbery? A gang-related attack? A police shoot-out?" I still did not know what was happening, but the sense of danger was obviously prevalent.

Attempting to run or even walk through the wild human pack would prove to be unsafe in or of itself anyway because people were already being trampled. I decided to look for people who were not going wild, as if in control, to identify them as possible assailants and start my journey in the opposite direction. I found no one fitting that description. Everybody seemed to be equally distressed and disconcerted. The assailants must have blended into the crowd to escape detection; a supposedly state-of-the-art security system was installed for the games.

As my hearing came back to life, I started to hear high-pitched sirens and commanding voices from what seemed to be official personnel. I could not really discern their exact meaning, but I was able to locate their source. One of the guards, voicing what seemed to be gibberish at the time, was leading the crowd and, while doing so, gesturing to calm down and walk out of the park. I then stood up and started walking really fast. For some reason, in the heat of the moment, I completely forgot about the numbness in my leg and magically regained complete control of it. I felt the sudden rush of adrenaline flowing through my body. I could hear the rapid palpitations of my heart as I went through the mob: "Thump, thump. Thump, thump." It also felt quite warm with little to no wind. Many more people than I anticipated were on the ground with spots of red on them and on the floor.

After what seemed to be an eternity, my frail leg abruptly gave way and I fell to the floor. For several seconds, I felt and saw persons of different shapes and sizes walk all over me. I felt the smooth curvature of bare feet and the clasp of stiff toes as well as the wrinkled rubber soles of sneakers as they impressed on my stomach a lasting sensation. My arms were unexpectedly stretched tight, almost out of their sockets, and my back started itching and burning. I figured I was being dragged somewhere. As I slightly raised my head forward, I saw my leg leave a trail of blood behind me on the asphalt. "I have been shot! Good GOD, I HAVE BEEN SHOT! I CANNOT BELIEEEeeevv."

"Explosives experts call it an 'anti-personnel fragmentation device,' but in Georgia, the pipe bomb that exploded in Centennial Olympic Park Saturday is an all-too-familiar instrument of terror. In Georgia, the pipe bomb has a long and murderous history as a low-tech tool of mayhem favored by white supremacists and other political extremists. . . . The bomb that exploded in the park Saturday was actually three pipe bombs packed with black gunpowder, nails and screws, sources told CNN. 'Essentially it's a pipe,' McGeorge said, 'a plain old plumbing pipe, threaded ends with caps screwed to both ends. The components are available in any hardware store in the country.' It could happen again. . . ."*

The television woke me. I was comfortable on my warm bed at home, under the covers. "Who brought me here?" The room looked as if nothing had happened, but the news obviously had something different to say. I looked to my right and saw that my clothes were on the laundry basket inside the walk-in closet, as I usually put them when I come home late. I was also in my usual pajamas. "After what happened, who could have brought me home who could have known of my living habits?"

I proceeded to uncover myself to examine the extent of the damage on my leg. I know now that flying shrapnel from a pipebomb inflicted the injury. Much to my surprise and astonishment, I saw no evidence of medical treatment! Under further scrutiny, I realized that no scars were present. "Wait a minute! I did go downtown and I did join the Olympic festivities! But that's *riiight!* I arrived home about two in the morning. That is when I watched the news and heard about the bomb that exploded half an hour after I left Centennial Olympic Park." A tragedy that I almost, if not implicitly, experienced in its entirety!

*Ann Kellan et al, "Pipe bombs: low-tech, lethal tools of terror," Web posted on: *http://cnn.com/US/9607/27/pipe.bomb.explain/index.html* at 10:25 P.M. EDT July 27, 1996.

"I THINK, THEREFORE I AM," Descartes says. But, in knowing that I am, as he proves, I really do not know if I am living reality or nearly dreaming it!

A Night of Bliss! Or Was It?

Diary,

I am confused. The story I am about to write is as true to me as anything in my life has ever been. It started on a Saturday morning and what a glorious day that was! I was in New Orleans, and I had some time to spare. Don's wedding, the reason behind my trip, was scheduled for four o'clock in the afternoon, and at the time it was only about ten in the morning. I walked out from the lobby of the *Fairmont Hotel,* a very beautiful and ornate establishment, onto *Canal Street* on my way to the *French Quarter.* Keith, another buddy, and I were on our way to meet a girl he met on the plane-ride into town. Her name was Pam.

The walk in and of itself was very colorful and rich in texture. The sweet smell of roses and the refreshing look of live ferns somehow meshed into the foul odor of trash and the stench from motor oil. The sidewalk in front of traditional two-story homes adorned with wrought-iron arches and time-honored Southern-looking windows was bordered with empty beer cans, banana peels, and grease-stained asphalt. The walk, overall, probably took about twenty to thirty minutes. Once we got to *Le Richelieu,* her hotel, which was also the hotel where the wedding party resided, we called her down.

Once Pam joined us, off to a bar we went. Its name was *Napoleon House Bar and Café.* We started with a great tasting yellowish drink, whose name escapes me at the moment. We had their infamous *Muffaletta* to go with it, which is a big round Italian sandwich dressed with olive oil. A few more drinks followed before we decided to head out to other spots in town. We walked through *Jackson Square* where I almost got bird droppings splashed on my bare left foot; I say bare because I was only wearing sandals. Street performers, painters, and human statues decorated the plaza. Birds, of course, flocked everywhere. We walked and talked for a while. Eventually, Pam had to leave us for an appointment with a masseuse.

"When will you be done with the wedding?" she asked.

"I don't really know, but we can meet somewhere at eleven-thirty in the evening!"

"Let's do that; how about *Le Pittsbsst on Bourbon Street?*"

"That sounds great!"

It was now right about two-thirty and we happened to stand right in front of *Jimmy Buffett's Margaritaville. Storyville* was the name of the bar, within *Margaritaville* that is, where we parked our mouths to drink some *Margaritas.* A piano player sang his heart out while we drank freely. Funky jazzy tunes flowed through the bar like ripples propagate in a still pond. People's voices could be distinguished over the music, but the words sounded like mere gibberish. It was after a while of admiring beautiful women, drinking *Margaritas,* and listening to great jazz that we realized we had to go back and get ready for the wedding.

We got to the hotel about twenty minutes after three in the afternoon. We were all sweaty and sticky from our long exposure to the sun. It must have been at least ninety degrees Fahrenheit. Since the wedding started at four, we had no time to take a shower. In fact, we barely had time to clean up and suit up. Well, we made it to the wedding right at four o'clock. The ceremony finished quickly and at about a quarter before five, we were already celebrating with *Champagne* in the *Paul McCartney Room.* While drinking, we made plans to go to *Pat O'Brien's Bar on St. Peter Street* to drink and party some more.

Well, we got to *Pat O's* after we changed into more comfortable clothing and started to drink again. I started off this time with a *Cuba Libre.* Some of the others started with *Hurricanes,* the infamous drink from *Pat O's.* Eventually, I too had Hurricanes. We were seated, unfortunately, in a drinks-only area, which meant that we could not order food. Oh, well, hard liquor sufficed for the moment. It was about time to meet Pam when we decided to venture out with most of the wedding crew to another bar, the bar where Pam was to wait for us. It was past eleven o'clock. On our way there, the streets were in party chaos. It was the *Southern Decadence,* which is the weekend where gays come together and celebrate. They were barely dressed, I must say. One guy dressed up with only a condom on his penis, a leather hat, and a pair of boots. Other guys walked hand in hand wearing nothing but thong leather underwear or string bikinis.

Bourbon Street was insane! People lined up all over the street and throughout a second-story porch to scream, drink, and celebrate. This all happened by *Oz,* a dance club. The minority of the bunch, a few other folks and us, were straight heterosexuals walking through an otherwise gay affair while observing and, of course, drinking beer and hard liquor out of our "take-out cups." I have never seen so much bare yet decorated male flesh all in one place. None of them, however, bothered us nor did we them.

Within a block's distance, we were back in "straightville." Women again glorified the streets with their voluptuous presence. Strip joints and band-filled bars were now everywhere. All of a sudden, we saw Pam walk by and we stopped her to chat. She was with some other guy and was already in a party mood. During this encounter, we inadvertently broke off from the wedding crew and lost contact. We talked with Pam for a while but eventually headed our own way.

We did not walk long before we encountered another exciting spot. As with the gays, a corner filled with people from all walks of life *partied like it was 1999,* AND 1999 IT WAS! Women on the porch of the second floor flashed their perfectly round milky-white breasts for a collar of beads. Some women were pretty enough to negotiate the type of beads they would get as well as the quantity. Some of the others, however, were not and thus revealed their bosoms at the slightest sign of a request. Others reveled in teasing the crowd by negotiating a bead price but never settling.

"Show us them t-ts!" the crowd yelled while pointing to a gorgeous blonde.

She would eventually give in by pulling up her blouse for two to three seconds. When she actually did this coveted act, someone, out of nowhere, shone a spotlight of some sort on her, showing the crowd the diva that she was. Horns, whistles, and sighs were heard during this momentous occasion. Needless to say, Keith and I camped out to enjoy the festivities. Drunks, perverts, winos, college kids, suits, and party animals were all pretty much the same. After a while, the women were mostly teasing and part of the hardcore crowd subsided. Well, on to the next stop we went.

We ended up catching the end of a concert at the *House of Blues on Decatur Street.* What a concert! We ordered beers and enjoyed the music. It was raunchy jazz in a somewhat intimate environment, a dark concert stage surrounded by bar stools and tables on two levels. There was a dance floor right in front of the stage filled with people dancing. Most of them paraded with a drink in their hand. To hold a conversation was futile and out of place. Bodies could barely stand still. The music could not help but inspire the very roots of anybody's soul. After listening to the last songs and walking around for a quick tour, we left and continued our pointless and aimless journey through time.

As we walked past a couple of strip joints, we saw a bar filled to the rim with patrons. A band was playing jazz and holding some sort of contest that drowned everybody's attention. Not lacking in party spirits, we joined to partake in the event. In walking through the crowd, I could hear the musician yell out: "SHOW US YOUR T-TS, BABY!"

When I finally got sufficiently close, I saw a perfectly fit girl, from the crowd, in tight black spandex pants shaking her booty on center stage. She reached under her skin-tight blouse to expose a beautiful black embroidered bra. After lifting her blouse just above her breasts, she clenched the underwire of her double-D bra and pulled it up to reveal her priceless jewels. Then, she turned around and pulled down her black pair of spandex pants. She gave the rest of the crowd, including myself, a full view of her bare behind with only a thin string riding up the creased river of love. Remember that this was just a girl from the crowd! She must have been twenty years old.

Soon after, the singer said: "Mom! It's your turn, honey!"

A woman in her early forties walked up to the stage and started to dance sensually. The previous girl then walked up to the stage again and lifted up the other woman's short one-piece dress. They embraced while their breasts smashed against one another. That was the girl's mom! She was also very pretty. "Mom" gave each of the musicians a private dance full of friction in all the sensitive spots. Like the daughter, she showed the crowd her boobs as well as her white butt.

Among the other contestants, there were two women in their mid-thirties who took the stage by storm. They were at the bar with their husbands and told the musicians they had small children at home. In any case, the brunette pulled up her red hot dress and the blond pulled up her short black skirt to show their goodies while dancing to a funky beat filled with sexual undertones. They danced back-to-back, rubbing each other's butts while showing the crowd their pleasing panties. It was wild! The crowd cheered and the contestants were simply having a blast! In the end, a girl who claimed to be from *Istanbul* won the contest. She had beautiful breasts, with perfectly tanned skin and curly dark brown hair. Had I been the only judge, I would have given the prize to the mom and daughter tag-team duo.

We stopped at a couple of other bars that also had music and impromptu beauty pageants. The only violence that we witnessed along the way was the beating of a red-bearded man. He was drinking beer when a black sport-utility vehicle drove by. Somehow the beer spilled as a result. "Red" decided to take revenge and threw an empty beer bottle at the car. He missed! He was in no shape to hit any target. Well, he pursued the car until he caught up and kicked it so hard that the echo reverberated throughout the block. The car abruptly stopped, and three black men flashed out, running around the car and converging on the frail assailant. They kicked him and punched him senseless. It was all over in less than ten seconds. All for a dollar's worth of beer and a stupid sense of pride! Yes, beer was sold for a dollar a cup on the street!

At this point is where my memory fades and images blur. Keith and I finally got back to *Canal Street*. There were many people dressed up in costumes with red and blue highlights. The music heard on the street became incoherent and muffled. Next thing I knew, I woke up in a small room with a television set on a long table and a Bible on a small nightstand by a dimly lit lamp. I was obviously in a motel. As I moved to get out of bed, I felt tremendous pain in my stomach. I pulled up the torn white tee-shirt I was wearing, and I saw bruises all over my abdomen. I could barely move without causing a great deal of agonizing pain. I dragged myself to the door across the worn-out carpet and walked out to the lobby of the motel. I felt my feet tight and saw that they were red and swollen. My arms also felt sticky. I had dried old beer all over my arms and legs.

"Where am I?" I asked.

"This is The Will———Motel on *Route 12*."

"Is this New Orleans?"

"Nope, we are about two hundred miles from there."

"How did I get here anyway? Did someone bring me?"

"I don't know. It wasn't my shift when you checked in. All I know is someone signed the guest book at eleven o'clock this morning."

After talking with the clerk, I took a shower, paid my bill, caught a taxi back to New Orleans, and flew back home. A few days later, I asked Keith if he knew what had transpired towards the end of that eventful night, but his memory was even shadier than mine was. All he said was:

"I woke up on a bench by a bus stop on *Canal Street.* I was very hung over! I went to the hotel after that and packed to go to the airport! I figured you had already left."

It is a week after, and my body is still aching all over. I am going to get checked out by the doctor tomorrow. I am afraid.

Who the Heck Knows?

It was Thursday morning, and Fabian woke up, like always, at six-thirty sharp. His morning routine consists of reading a chapter from his favorite book, working out, showering, and eating breakfast. By eight o'clock, he is usually in his car and on his way to work. The main agenda for today, in particular, was to give a presentation at work and to go out on a date that evening. He was to present a detailed account of the history of a diversified portfolio of stocks and mutual funds. Fabian is a market research analyst. He felt pretty confident about his presentation since he knew the material inside and out. Needless to say, the presentation went without a hitch. His boss was greatly impressed.

Eight o'clock in the evening rolled by and Fabian was ready for his date. He was nervous. The woman's name was Michele, and this occasion would mark their second encounter. Oscar, Fabian's college buddy, had introduced Michele to Fabian a few days earlier. In preparation for the much-anticipated event, Fabian rehearsed what his first line would be and how he would recite it. He thought on how and when he would hold her hand and at what point he would wrap his arm around her. He even wrote down on a small piece of paper a few topics of conversation that he would use in case the dialogue dried out to dreadful silence.

The date ended up being a bust! He was awkward from the very start. He literally stumbled and almost fell to the pavement while leading Michele into the car. The incident made him blush. "*Oh, MAN!*" was all he said. Two minutes into the date, while still in the car, they already ran out of things to talk about.

"How about them Dolphins!" he said in an attempt to sparkle up a conversation. "That is only my favorite professional football team. Do you follow any sports?"

"Not really. I am more into movies, music, and theatre. I like to paint a little also. But sports, they don't really attract me as much."

"Really. That's interesting."

Fabian panicked! From that point on, he could not think of anything else to say. Art was not a topic that he rehearsed, and he was too nervous to improvise any intelligible comments on the subject. Unfortunately, but expectedly of course, the rest of the evening proved to be no different. After dinner, he took Michelle home and ended the date with a very cold, tense, and hesitant kiss on the cheek.

That Saturday Fabian was going to play in a volleyball tournament. He ate pasta the night before to supply him with carbohydrates, energy. He also stocked up on bananas. They would provide him with potassium to help prevent cramps during the games. Before the competition, he felt rested and fully energized. He, drowned with adrenaline and full of physical composure, felt as good as ever! As the day went on, his team proved to be unbeatable. They all clicked. Fabian was simply flying all over the court; he was able to return any spike while dishing out kills left and right. His legs did not cramp and his body did not waver. Talk about a perfect day!

Sunday morning, while still in bed, Fabian had a few moments to reflect and thought to himself: *I felt good and ready for my lecture and my tourney and they turned out great. On the other hand, I felt tentative and self-conscious for my date and it crashed. Oh well, such is my dating life!*

Monday came and, from the time that Fabian woke up in the morning, he just knew that it would be a bad day. Sure enough, the milk was spoiled; he could not find his brown dress shoes; his white Mustang stalled, and, bad news awaited him at the office: a project gone haywire. Throughout the day Fabian basically knew what would happen before it actually occurred. Some people chug this type of premonition to the reality of *Murphy's Law*. This, however, was a bit more than that. Fabian knew exactly what negative reaction his boss would have at his every comment.

By three o'clock in the afternoon. Fabian realized that he better start telling people exactly what they wanted to hear or rather how they wanted to hear it for his own sake. Since he knew what their reaction would be beforehand, he could communicate in a manner that always elicited a positive response from his co-workers and anyone who happened to interact with him.

I have arranged for Margo to give you the reports first thing in the morning. I will be out taking care of my car; it needs some work to run like a champ again. By the way, the report shows a fall in the price of the stock, but I project a quick recovery before the end of the week.

Tuesday was more of the same. Fabian expected everything to go well and, as if by magic, everything did go well. The car was fixed. The value of the stock, the one referenced in his report, went up. His report was right on the money! Everybody in the office eagerly greeted him with enthusiasm and affection. He just knew, somehow, that everyone would be positive and insightful.

Around four o'clock, he thought about traveling to Europe with a volleyball team. A few minutes later, he found an opportunity in his monthly volleyball newsletter. "The opportunity of a lifetime," it said, "a tour of Europe with an adult volleyball team. Sightsee and play at the same time!" How eerie! Something as out in left field as that could actually become a reality. He called the coach, got a phone interview, and a personal tryout. He had made the team!

The following week, on Tuesday night, he was telling his friend Carl how great these past couple of weeks had been for him and how sure he was that it would stay that way. Carl replied with: "That is great! My life, on the other hand, is not so perfect. I guess it isn't too bad either. I am glad for you though."

Fabian found similar responses from everyone he met. For some reason the stars seemed to be lined up just right for him. Still, despite the uniqueness of his situation, his confidence did not falter. He was still in control.

One night he had a wonderful dream. He was eating dinner with his girlfriend, a stunningly attractive and engaging brunette. They were enjoying a meal with Fabian's parents who came to visit from their home in Key West, Florida. They were having a delightful evening full of friendly affectionate smiles and stimulating conversations. They were on the outdoor patio of a beautifully ornate restaurant. The weather was perfect: sunny with a cool soft breeze. He woke up the next morning and ended up meeting a gorgeous woman in the elevator on his way to his office. He had a wonderful impromptu date that evening. The following day Fabian's parents called to announce their intent to visit a week from Friday. his dream seemed to be turning into reality!

"RRRRRRRiinnnnnnnng!" The alarm cheered. Fabian, still half-asleep, was a bit unsure of the timeline.

"Is it Wednesday or Thursday? It doesn't really matter, I guess. I know I still have to go to work anyway," he murmured to himself.

His mom called him at work later on and asked him if it would be okay to visit him on Friday.

"Of course, Mom! I look forward to it. Didn't you already tell me about this, though?"

"No! Your dad and I just spoke of it this morning and only decided THEN to go."

"How weird! I guess I dreamt it."

This puzzled him a bit. He knew, though, that his date that night with Claudia, the gorgeous woman from the elevator, was real. Well, they met at the movie theatre later that evening. They took in a movie and ate dinner afterwards. They spent the night together and slept in passionate bliss.

"RRRRRRRiinnnnnnnng!" Another day! He woke up, got ready for work, and drove to work. The traffic was light, and he arrived at work in no time. As he entered the office, he thought about the wonderful night he had with Claudia. All of a sudden, it struck him that he did not see Claudia in the morning. "Oh well, she probably went to work early." At noon, he got a phone call.

"Hello, Fabian speaking!" he uttered as he picked up the phone.
"Good morning, honey! It's your mom!"
"Good morning, Mom! Is everything going well? How is Dad?"
"Everything is great! I just wanted to ask you if it would be all right if your dad and I visited you this Friday? Do you have any plans?"
"MOM! You've already asked me! Don't you remember?"
"Impossible. Your dad and I have been vacationing all week and we've been away from telephones."
"WHAT! Wait a minute! Did I dream it then? Perhaps I am dreaming this. Maybe I dreamt your last call."
"Stop the nonsense. I don't have time for games, sweetheart."

How could he tell, though? Fabian found himself totally confused. Did he altogether dream the past two weeks? Was he still dreaming?

"How do I know that I am not dreaming this call, Mom?"
"Because I am telling you that you are not. After all, I am talking with you!"
"You could have the same reaction in my dream. That somewhat discredits your reassurance, doesn't it?"

"Have you been getting enough sleep?"

"YES. Anyway, let me hang up and get to work. By the way, I
    have made plans to spend the weekend, including Friday,
    with you guys. See you then. Bye, Mom!"

"Get some rest! Good-bye, baby!"

Fabian could not get any work done that day. He started to reflect on these past few weeks and how he had been able to do well in every aspect. He thought about his uncanny ability to predict people's reaction and his impeccable intuition. He reflected on how it was that his date with Michele bombed and how he could have foretold its outcome by merely looking at his attitude before the date even began. How was it that the opportunity to go to Europe presented itself right after he contemplated the idea? He thought on how he believed, at one point in his life, that going for a master's degree would be too difficult. When he did try it, the task became literally impossible to handle despite everyone else's confidence in his ability to do it. How relaxed and confident he was in high school when he tried for the volleyball team and how he not only made the team but also proved to be the star player. He also thought about how distressed he was his first two years of college. he was taking a full load of classes and working part time as a pizza deliveryman. He knew that he had little time to practice volleyball and felt out of shape but still tried out for the team. Despite his talent and stellar years in high school, he could not show his potential to the team and its coach.

I should have known I would not make the team! I did not feel I
could at the time. All my life I have been in control of my destiny
and I have not realized it! I have maneuvered every outcome and I
have designed every situation. I still cannot really tell if all of that
was a dream or not. Perhaps there is no difference between one and
the other. Why do oppositely charged particles attract? Why are
objects pulled to the ground? There is no justifiable reason! Is
there? The only evidence, electricity and gravity, simply indicate

that they do exist, but they don't explain why they exist. That is, they exist in my dream, in my world, or, better put, in my reality.

Is there any other reality? Possibly someone else's? Everybody else is a figment of my imagination, though. Is the human body the soul's temple? Well, if everybody else lives in my world, in a dream I created, I may just have devised everyone's persona after my own spitting image, the image I created of myself for myself. So, a human body is not necessarily attached to a soul. In fact, my true shape and my true form may not even be human. What is the human race anyway? My own creation, of course! Everything is my creation! The laws of physics, the physical and chemical limitations of biology, people's instincts and emotional reactions, my own abilities, the earth around me, the physical forces of nature, and miracles, they are all products of my imagination. I don't need sleep then. I don't really need to eat, walk, work, talk, or read.

Wow! With this revelation, Fabian suddenly found himself floating in black space. His five senses were no longer existent, were no longer an impediment. He was no longer there. All that was left was a black bottomless pit that ultimately ended in complete and absolute silence. Questions ceased and the word reality had no meaning. Fabian was no longer Fabian; in fact, he was no longer a "he" or even an "it." Everything was nothing and nothing was everything. Positive and negative infinity came full circle to converge onto a singular point, no time, no lines no two-dimensional planes, and not even three-dimensional space.

"RRRRRRRiinnnnnnng!"

"What! Where am I? Am I still dreaming or am I awake? Am I 'I'?"

Who the heck knows?

Ciao Romano!

Sweat built while adrenaline circulated like the Carolina Rapids. We, an American volleyball team, played against a local *Italian team,* a *Roman team.* Our cherished experience did not end on the court, though. After the excitement and the rush of the games subsided, we took pictures and made plans to celebrate our acquaintance at a local pizzeria. A table, probably made to seat approximately eighteen people, was barely sufficient to fit our rather large and vociferous crowd. I sat among five beautiful and gregarious women, four Italian and one American. Italian, Spanish, French, and English adorned our picturesque discussion. We ate, drank, partied, and joked all night. Our lively conversation ranged from translated clichés to arduous tales and practical gags. There must have been five different conversations going at once, and we all switched from one to the other with relative ease and comfort. No one was exempt from being the butt of a joke!

As our evening closed, late into the night, the Italian group gave us a ride back to our accommodations. Business cards and phone numbers were exchanged while the intensity of the celebration persisted. Finally, it was time for farewells. I welcomed the opportunity to adopt the Italian custom of kissing all the women, a well-received mandate in my book! I then went to shake the hands of the men when: "Wait! . . . *Mmuahh.* . . . What! . . . *Mmuahh.* . . . Again?" Time suddenly slowed and my body tensed. My brain was in dire need of a jumpstart! *He just kissed me on both cheeks!*

As my senses awakened, I regained control and was thusly able to conclude our send-off. I lingered in a clandestine daze all throughout the ceremonious *Ciao,* realizing, of course, the fortune just bestowed upon me, my induction into their fraternity of friendship!

King of the Beach!

It was some time ago when I competed in one of my most memorable tournaments, a sand doubles volleyball tournament with a "*King of the Beach*" format. The peculiarity of this particular format is that a player does not play with his own partner. Instead, his partner changes with every game. Ultimately the single best player, not the top team, wins the coveted title *King of the Beach.* Each individual's record is used to set the rankings. For instance, if a pool of four is formed, a player plays with each of the other three during the course of three consecutive games. Partners are rotated with each game. In the end, the person with the best record, in terms of wins and losses, places first and advances to the next bracket. If two players tie, the total number of points earned throughout the three games is used to establish a winner. As the players advance, they get to play with other bracket winners until eventually advancing to the finals where the best four compete for first and second place.

There are several aspects I like about a tournament of the sort. The idea of competing as an individual athlete in a sport that is necessarily team-oriented appeals to me. It forces a player to work on every facet of the game. One cannot rely on a partner to compensate for one's own shortcomings. I also enjoy meeting and playing with other dedicated players not to mention the thrill of the challenge in it of itself.

This tournament in particular was held sometime in May, I think, in the middle of the brutal Texas heat. It started in the morning, somewhere around ten o'clock, and lasted all day. I was placed in a pool of four players. The brackets were such that the top two competitors from each pool advanced. Additionally, two wild cards also advanced. The wild cards are the next best two players among all the existing pools. The ranking is based, of course, on the player's performance through the first pool. I do not remember how many pools there were, but my focus, at the time, was simply to play each game as it came without regards to the other players and their respective games. I was pumped and psyched to play and compete. This was my first sand volleyball tournament of the season.

The skill level of the players in my specific pool was pretty much even, excepting one player. He was more of a *B-player* than an *A-player,* relatively speaking. As it might be guessed, whoever played with this guy lost the match. As a result, the other two players and I had two wins and one loss each. Imagine, a three-way tie! Unfortunately, when it came to total points won, I placed third and only the first two qualified. That meant I did not automatically advance. I had to wait until all the other pools finished their respective games to allow the official to determine the identity of the wild cards.

The pools finished and I approached the official table, or I should say the official bench, to ascertain my ranking. At this point, I did not really want to stop playing and I found myself obsessing over the results and the final standings. Awaiting my fate while others played was a test of my patience and waiting longer became unbearable. As numbers were crunched and names were tossed, I started to realize that I had a fighting chance. Finally, I was told I was the first wild card to make it. *Great news,* I thought. I barely advanced but I did do it nonetheless.

Well, another pool was assembled and a court was assigned. I played with a new set of players in a pool of four. By now, the sun was working overtime while the clouds were apparently taking a long nap. We were to play on Court Three. Among us there was a skilled player who tended to place the ball well around the court and right on the lines. He did not spike much, but he really did not have the need to do it. The other two and I were competitively even. Based on the results of the previous pool, I would have expected, perhaps, that whoever played with the trickster would win since he was good. The scenario certainly started fulfill its prophecy. The trickster won the first two games. The third game, however, did not turn out quite the same way. The trickster lost by two points. Luckily, I was a member of the opposing team. The trickster placed first, but we had a two-way tie for second. Alas, we ran into a minor problem. A guy and I tied in games and in points!

We were told to *dual it out* in a one-on-one game to seven points, winning by at least two points. The court would be divided in two, and each player would bump, set, and spike all by himself. How weird! The size of the court ended up being approximately four and a half by eighteen meters. It was still a lot of ground to cover for just one measly player. Off we went, though. Serving to a court half wide with an unsteady wind is difficult enough, but to realize that the game decided our fate made the task nerve-racking and, quite frankly, somewhat stressful. At this point, of course, I had a thick layer of sand all over my body from diving on the court. The sand stuck to my skin like spandex. The thick mix of sweat and suntan lotion created the perfect *sand trap.*

I tried to play one point at a time and forget about the ultimate implications of each serve, pass, set, and spike. I won with a score of something like seven/five. What a relief! Strike that, what a glorious conclusion. I, again, barely advanced by the mere *skin of my teeth.* This time I legitimately advanced to the loser's bracket. Whoever placed first in their pool, at this stage of the tournament, made it to the winner's bracket, which meant that they had a *bye.* The folks in the loser's bracket, like myself, had to play and advance once more before they could play in the finals. The players in the winner's bracket, on the other hand, automatically made it to the finals.

It was now about two o'clock in the afternoon. Normally, I do not like to eat much throughout a tournament because the food tends to weigh heavily in my stomach. I eat light snacks and drink plenty of liquids to keep hydrated. Much to my dismay though, I already finished, perhaps even sweated out, my gallon's worth of refreshing tea. A fellow player shared his sports drink with me. My body was definitely grateful for his sportsmanship. Anyway, we started to play our next set of games. Mental and physical conditioning certainly started to play a bigger role in the games. We were getting tired, and the sun continued to glow and swarm us with intense and unadulterated heat. Games one, two, and three came and went and I managed, somehow, to end up second in the pool. I could not believe it. I did not have to dual out another tie to advance. I had made it to the finals!

Among the four finalists, I played the most games since I consistently advanced in last place and even played a tiebreaker game. I was beginning to feel my thighs and calves tingle from exhaustion. But, as there is never time to waste, we started to play our final three games. As may be expected, I felt shocks of electricity flow through my tiring arms and back as they threatened to ignite muscle cramps in a dominolike fashion. The condition climaxed during my first game of the finals when my right calf momentarily cramped while jumping for a spike. Each time I would jump thereafter, it would cramp again. I communicated this to my partner, my partner for that match that is, saying that I should not receive the ball first since doing so would force me to spike. Letting my partner pass and spike the ball would allow me to simply set, which is decisively less strenuous on the calves. Unfortunately, we lost that match.

Since cramps, for the most part, result from dehydration and lack of potassium, I usually bring bananas in my bag to supplement me with potassium. I normally use it as a preventive measure. This time, however, I needed it for its curing powers. If my condition persisted, my last partner, now my adversary, would have most likely exploited my weakness. After swallowing down half a banana in a single chug, I felt better. In fact, I could actually jump again, or so it seemed!

As it turned out, there was a player who was obviously better than the rest of us. From the little that I had now seen and heard, he easily advanced within the winner's bracket all day. Anyone who played with him won the game. The challenge was to accumulate more points than the remaining two finalists to be able to end up in second place. Well, I did not play with him on either the first or the second game, which meant that I lost both. On the third game, I played with him and by now I could figure out how many points it would take for the opposing team to displace me from second place. I could not allow them to win more than three points for me to finish second or more than four points for me to tie for second.

Points came and went before the score momentarily settled to nine/three. I was already at the brink of losing. A point, unfortunately, slipped from my grasp and the score became nine/four. Talk about a mental challenge! I was disappointed but I still had a chance. I do not know how, but my partner and I pulled it off and won without letting them get any additional points. He was gracious enough to go all out even after being tired and knowing in fact that he would win first place regardless of the score and much less the margin.

The crusade did not end here. Now we had a first-place winner and a tie for second. Unfortunately, only two prizes were available, so second place had to be determined. Guess what! Another tiebreaker game had to be played. Like before, this would be one-on-one and on half a court. It was now past four o'clock and the sun, of course, gleamed with infinite radiance. I gulped down the other half of my last banana to prepare myself, but its effectiveness was diminishing with each passing minute. I could not allow us to wait too long because my muscles would certainly cramp up otherwise. This game was my fourteenth! Wow! I wanted to win it badly too. After such a long day, I could almost smell the sweet odor of victory. By now, my body was basically running on fumes.

After what seemed to be a very long game, I miraculously won the game! My muscles twitched in disbelief as my very essence remained in shock. I placed second in the tournament.

I am not a professional player nor am I an Olympic-caliber athlete by any stretch of the imagination. In fact, I have a day job that provides me with a good income and playing volleyball is simply entertainment and exercise. However, I cannot convey how much the fifteen-dollar gift certificate, the ultimate prize for first and second place, meant and still means to me. I am almost justified in claiming that I became a professional player that day. After all, I actually earned money for playing volleyball, fifteen bucks for a day's work!

El Temible Gatillo

Pintura de Palabras:

En el panorama se destaca una malla negra de tres cuartos de metro de altura con sobre-borde blanco, y elevada del piso aproximadamente dos metros. Ella se extiende interminablemente a todo lo largo del horizonte. Encima de esta cortina rùstica de cuerdas se encuentran cuatro brazos, largos y extendidos, con las manos abiertas y unidas una a la otra formando así una pared de carne impenetrable.

Un poco a la derecha y al fondo se ve una figura a través de la red cuadriculada. Este personaje es un leal defensor que esta casi arrodillado en el suelo con los pies bien plantados y los muslos tensos dándole un balánce casi perfecto, como animal listo para reaccionar a cualquier amenaza repentina. Sus manos la tiene a la altura del ombligo, encerradas en una ensalada de digitos, amarrados en nudos. Los brazos, naciendo del cuerpo, se extienden al punto de casi tocar el piso. Su cara esta borrosa y fuera de foco pero todo su ser se dirige hacia la dirección del protagonista. Atrás de este jugador y un poco a su derecha hay otra imagen, la de otro soldado en posición similar. Cada uno, claro esta, defiende su perimetro que forma parte integral del flanco derecho. Al final, ellos ayudan a proteger el cuartel. A la izquierda de los cuatro brazos, sobre la malla, se encuentra una franja negra bordando el campo. Entre esta linea negra y los brazos, solo hay un camino estrecho, una calle ciega terminada por otro defensor.

Este, como sus compañeros del otro flanco, esta preparado para el inevitable y esperado ataque.

Hacia arriba y un poco a la derecha de la pared humana, hay una pelota flotando en el aire en su trayectoria hacia el protagonista, proviniendo de su mismo lado de la malla y siendo colocada por un compatriota. Los ojos del protagonista, estando a un nivel un poco mas alto de la malla, coinciden con el punto de vista de la obra, y cuyo punto de foco intrinseco es el balón que se encuentra un poco adelante y a la derecha. Otro compañero, agresor también, esta en pleno vuelo, justo a su derecha. Su empeño y su destreza intíma que le va a pegar a la pelota con anhelo y pasión. Pero, por el ángulo y altura de aquella bomba, es al protagonista a quien le toca disparar el cañón. El, como su camarada, también esta en el aire con el brazo derecho atrás y encima de la cabeza, y el hombro izquierdo adelante, y al nivel de la cara. La mano izquierda encuentra su posición apuntando hacia el balón ambulante, anticipando así el desenlace del látigo cuya punta venenosa es, nada mas y nada menos, que la otra mano, ¡el temible gatillo!

POEMS

Weeping in Tears of Mud!

Dwindling Light
Fading Souls
Forceful Flight
Dead Corridor

Rain of Tears
March of Shock
Sea of Fear
Tomb of Hopes

Piercing Pain
Burning Rage
Clenching Veins
Paralyzing Migraine

Sinful Destruction
Fatal Calamity
Horrific Annihilation
Brutal Reality

Dreaded December sixteen
Lifeless morning
Rude awakening
MI VENEZUELA IN MOURNING

Strawberry Delight

The wind whistled and forcefully blew;
The sails could only obey tight, snug, and blue.

The water crashed hard against the hull;
It exploded into a thousand golf balls as a result.

The jumpy crew hustled throughout the eve,
But the lofty sheets were hard to please.

The Caribbean, of course, didn't surrender;
She staked her ground with unyielding splendor.

*   *   *

Just when the light of hope began to fade,
The eye of the storm approached and waved.

The skies above wrestled with thundering might,
Still in my arms she anchored in a single flight.

With the swift blink of a tiring eye,
Nirvana took her hostage to another place and time.

She floated me away in quiet hymns and glorious lights,
I slowly drowned in strawberry delight.

Dusk

A spear of lightning stabs my shriveled heart.
It twists and turns from left to right.

The nights lengthen with unceasing want.
My spirit plummets without hope or regard.

My lips shake and my hands tremble at the frozen light.
My sight blurs in the middle of the fight.

Pain dwells deep within where the soul begins.
Yell I must, yet my tongue can hardly move or impinge.

Tears trickle down my sea of despair.
My chest explodes a thousand times without any air.

Ashes die and dirt turns to dust.
I fade into the abyss of dusk.

Ojitos Verdes

Esa magia que despiertan las estrellos fugaces al volar el cielo
infinito

Esa ternura, plena, y pura, que exprime el alma y hala de punta

La dulzura misma, hecha de miel y de azucar, con colores
blancos y almohadones de pluma

Calor perfecto, de otoño al mediodia, que no quema y siempre
suaviza

Girasol de terciopelo, amarillo y rosado, que acaricia sin saber y
anima al solo ver

Espíritu ambulante que oasis en marmolina sin sol me brinda

Mamita, la de ojitos verdes que pinta esta tinta sincera y en lujo
de rima

D. C. in Whites

The white curtain closed and I looked

Coats and gloves walked and ice grew

One thousand flakes strong came down and then anew

A soft bed of foam arose and with glue

Visions of milk-drenched cotton in everything but stew

City of lights suited with gowns of frost and hue

Angelic stardust falling from the sky into our moon-lit brew

Oh, I'm in heaven and I never knew!

Open the Shutter!

How do I let God in my life?
    I was once asked in the mist.
I turned my head slowly and eagerly answered this,
    My only recipe to undying bliss:

I open my shutter and I open it wide
I let the light shine bright and I let it inside

It fills my abyss with angels of delight
It warms my bones and it rejuvenates them right

Company it brings with a thousand twinkling stars
Beauty it exudes and poetry it sparks

Loneliness then desists and perfect harmony insists
Purpose and meaning ultimately result and coexist

All this I get when my camera opens its shutter from left to right
When my soul welcomes the sun and ends the night

I now live all of this, day in and day out,
All because I realized God is always within and never without

My Gift to You

I got this little something for you
It is a pack of words I chose to use
For the whole purpose of bringing me to you
When you are feeling alone or blue.

The topics are varied and true
From a child's tale to a romantic woo
Even an occasional game of words is included in the loot
Ornate paintings borrowed from other people's brew

Think of me when you read this through
For I will be there right by you
Time, space, and physics will cease to rule
Once these words swiftly float out of you

Itch for the Ultimate Thrill!

My stomach itched with unceasing want
It longed for something but certainly not bread or wine

My soul screamed tears of pain
All it wanted was another taste of hell

Thrills of crushing fear and certain dread
Left nothing but yearn for more and frustrating rage

Climbing, rafting, and skydiving were only in part
Exotic beds and tingling delight also filled the nights

A rocky road, drowned in adrenaline and lit in sparks,
Was paved and carved in vain each passing night

My appetite grew and could not be quenched
Until I finally saw the light on September eighth

I checked out that morning and left a lifeless corpse
Only to plunge into death with unmitigated force

Sheets

They're the rose petals, soft and sweet,
that swiftly land on my chest and knees.

Staggered in time and with commanding peace
they float up and down with amazing ease.

They caress the skin from neck to toe
as if softly sculpting in pure fresh fallen snow.

"They are only sheets!" I could have said
not really knowing one white from another red.

It's only now that I can see
the true joy of falling asleep!

Caribbean Rose

It was a beautiful Caribbean night when it all started:

A cosmic voyage of lights and stars
A rainbow of sweet chocolates and the like
A page inspired in gold and angels alike
The sweet aroma of red roses in late March

We carved it all in infinite faith
And today we opted to turn the page
The sculpture, however, will never fade
And the memories will forever live in spades

So, farewell for now; we will surely meet again
Maybe not tomorrow or the next day
And not even as lovers or as mates
But the day will come and we will dine 'til late

Ciao, sweet rose, my sweet Caribbean friend!

The Church

It's a dark place I go on Sunday nights
    We call it The Church but only when the time is right
Everyone dresses in black and in the flesh
    Some with leather boots and others with silk capes

The lights are always dim
    With a hint of somber grins
The music throughout is loud
    And so is the melancholy crowd

Rings of all sorts proudly hail
    They parade on noses, tongues, nipples, and in ale
Makeup ranges from pale white to black and red
    And silver chains adorn the mesh

Dancing is nothing short of bliss
    Where everyone surrenders to the natural flow of hiss
Some move fast and jump quick
    While others take delight in hovering in the mist

A bunch of freaks the norm seems to see
    Bad seeds born of earth and sea
We are certainly different and distinct
    And we like to think of ourselves as we

We care for life, dirt, and speed
    We do nothing wrong except for being free
We celebrate diversity and rejoice in deeds
    And avoid settling in old patterns of creed

We are sons and daughters
    Who play at night to recover
We are also students and part of the workforce
    With our own ideals and love for our mothers

We accept and respect the norm
    But freedom we ask in the name of the Lord
Let us be and judge us not
    We are like you, only unique and sometimes quite bold

Mi Madrileña

What a perfect night that was
    Madrid has never been so exquisite, not in the past
The sky was clear, pure, and dark blue
    Three quarters of the moon sparkled in radiant
    hymns of hue
The tireless city played its tune six floors below
    A sweet medley of hushed sounds made it glow

Through the balcony doors I witnessed it all
    I could feel my heart bloom in response to the call
The curtains slowly danced and swiftly flew
    As the cool Spring air played its harmonic flute
Minutes, hours, and days could have passed
    Only to find themselves cycling back to the past

My Madrileña I beheld in my arms that night
    She was soft and sweet, not to mention warm and right
We celebrated with Spanish guitars and clapping palms
    And only finished in melodic psalms
I will never forget that glorious evening in Madrid
    When time and space ceased and I lived in bliss

A Pink Rose

Days come and go,
    Hours pass and people flow
This weekend, though,
    Time will stop and the moon will glow
The stars will dance
    And the birds will chant!

It isn't every day that a rose is born
    A pink one, no less, with sweet flesh tones
She is the star of this summer sky!
    A tribute to beauty and all flowers alike
She comes to us by way of luck and through chance
    Only to beautify it all with her charm!

She is, of course, the inspiration of this short verse
    One heartfelt dedication to her gleaming grace!